KAREN CLARK-GREEN

THE CURSE OF THE STRONG WOMAN

*What God Expects From Godly Women
In the Last Days*

Copyright © 1996 by Karen Clark-Green
Revised May, 2002 by Karen Clark-Green

All rights reserved. All quotations in this book are divinely inspired and therefore written permission must be secured from the publisher to use or reproduce any part of this book, except for brief quotation in critical reviews or articles.

Published in Youngstown, Ohio, by Omega Publishing House, Inc., 4870 Brookwood Rd. Suite 2, Boardman, Ohio 44512 phone 330.782.4995 and distributed in the United States by Archangel Ministries, P.O. Box 116, Youngstown, Ohio 44501, e-mail address - mudalev@yahoo.com

Printed by Calvary Publications
Printed in the United States of America.

Scripture quotations, unless otherwise noted, are from THE KING JAMES VERSION of the Bible, Copyright © 1979, 1980, 1982, Thompson Chain-Reference Bible, Inc.

ISBN: 1-886297-21-5

Clark-Green, Karen
The Curse of The Strong Woman

Contents

Dedication 7
Acknowledgments 9
Preface 11
Introduction 13

Part One

The Importance of a Woman.. 15
1. Who Am I?... 19
2. The Woman's Covenant... 29

Part Two

The "Me" No One Knows... 33
3. Created Special 35
4. People Pleasing 37
5. The Power of Influence 41
6. The Missing Child 53

Part Three

The Strong Woman... 61
7 Change Your Mind 63
8 The Next Level 67
9 The Virtuous Woman -Who Can Find One? 73
10 The Lion and the Lamb 79
11 What You See Is What You Get 89

Part Four

The Curse 95
12 The Walking Dead 99
13 The Broken Heart 103
14 Eanie, Meanie, Minee, Mo, Will My Mate Be
      Friend or Foe? 115
15 What God Expects From Godly Women 127

Part Five

Free at Last 133
16 Spirit, Soul and Body 135
17 Happiness for the Whole Person 149
18 Walking in Authority 157

Conclusion - Elements in Review 161

DEDICATION

It is May 1, 2002 and I am rewriting the dedication of this book. I began to write this book in 1993, it was finished February of 1996. According to God's plan the book was held up for the next six years. So much has happened in my life during this time, but I recall the writing and research of this book as my therapy.

For the last year the Lord greatly impressed upon me to finish the task and that the book must be released. I originally dedicated this book to my husband, who recently passed on November 1, 2001 and to my father, who passed February 14, 1998.

I must now dedicate this book to the four beautiful children that the Lord gave to us; Michael, Jr., Paul Gabriel, Ebony Rose and Joshua William. I greatly acknowledge them for their endurance, support, patience and love while I walked into my healing and sought how to bring others with me.

Furthermore my Mother, who taught me perseverance and how to be strong. And my late maternal grandmother, the late Lenora Jackson Moss. She planted a seed of holiness in me without my knowledge, that took root and is now producing great things for God.

ACKNOWLEDGMENTS

To my good friend, Debra Kerr for working so hard to help me with the manuscript; thank you for your encouragement and for believing in my dreams and visions. You taught me that not only are my goals possible, they are inevitable!

A special thanks to: Sheila Hayes, Earli Burks, Jeanetta Pugh, Regina Hall-Barbour and Maestro William Slocum who has been there for every stage of my career. And a special thank you to Dr. Lawrence Simpson for your encouragement and patience.

PREFACE

It is so easy, particularly as women, to pull back or withdraw because of mistakes or painful memories. Maybe someone has hurt you so badly that you feel like you have been destroyed, and you have allowed yourself to retreat to the point of being captured. You are locked up tight and sealed in a box. Other people's likes, dislikes and expectations begin to rule your life.

We can allow our mistakes to rob us of our true identity, or we willingly give up and die. The mistake, sin or whatever the problem, can keep you from forgiving yourself.

The power and potential of the person that God created has now been robbed. Somewhere along the line of events, you allowed yourself to be taken over. You retreated and moved into a back room. The devil takes the keys, locks the door and something else begins to direct your life.

People who come in contact with you; your loved ones, your mate and children, usually reap pain because of your death. And in turn, the pain begins to kill them.

It is not premeditated, you may not be in control of anything that is happening but death is taking place nonetheless. You are tied up, gagged and can't do anything about it. Once you accept this, you can work the ropes free, pull the gag out of your mouth and use your authority to get your keys back. Let the real you go free so that you can begin to live your life. First, however, you must realize that this is the state that you are in to be totally set free.

INTRODUCTION

As women in the last days, we are faced with trials and test that have never existed before. To do God's will, we must become the individuals God has created us to be. What does God expect from us as women, especially in these last days? Is this time any different than any other time?

This message is to women. It is intricate and profound, and it will help you to get free to become the real you!

In a changing society, our roles as women have taken on new challenges. The quick changes in the last half of this century have expanded the roles of women. Women live longer, masses of wives and mothers are pursuing careers, and on top of all this, we have a call on our lives that God expects us to fulfill. We use to totally depend on our men to provide for us but now most of what they could provide, we can provide for ourselves.

Somewhere in my life, I made the decision that I would be the perfect wife and mother. I did not realize that I was setting myself up for defeat and emotional ruin.

Stress, depression and hopelessness were all masked by my strength. The ability to do my job, your job, the kids jobs and anyone else's job that didn't get done, robbed my life. As a result everything that I attempted to do would overwhelm me. My self esteem and confidence dropped along with my vitality. I doubted myself as an artist, mother, minister, teacher and then I began to believe that I was a failure at everything.

INTRODUCTION

Lack of self worth will cause you to consider everyone else first and yourself last. You will begin to feel trapped and believe that there is no way out. Peace and happiness will no longer be a part of your vocabulary.

I did not realize that my goals, sense of purpose and identity had been buried and that I had allowed them to be. Once you reach this state it will keep you in blind disobedience to God. We are living in a 'NOW' time, it is now time to do all that you were born to do. How do we start? Where is the beginning? You start by forgiving yourself and all others. Yes, you failed and you may fail again. Even in your failure, you have had some success, look at those and celebrate. Even though you thought that you would lose your mind, it is still in tact. Even though you said, "I can not make it through one more day, you made it!"

As you read this book, I believe you will begin to change. You will probably face some hard facts about yourself and those close to you. It is important that the real you becomes a reality and that you accomplish what is required of you, in these last **days.**

PART 1

THE IMPORTANCE OF A WOMAN

> *My frame was not hidden from you when I was being formed in secret [and] intricately and curiously wrought [as if embroidered with various colors] in the depths of the earth [a region of darkness and mystery].*
> **Psalm 139:15 AMP**

I was so excited to be able to share the stage with Maya Angelou, the featured speaker for Cuyahoga Community College's Martin Luther King Celebration. I was the featured soloist for the celebration with the Cleveland Philharmonic Orchestra. This performance was a step toward rebuilding an enriched life for me. A career I had closed the door on had reopened in such a grand way; all I had to do was have the courage to walk through.

The Curse of the Strong Woman   Karen Clark-Green

As I waited backstage, impatiently looking to get a glimpse of this great lady, she stepped from behind the backdrop. I had read her books and admired her love affair with the English language for so long. I never dreamed that I would be sharing a stage with her. I had always considered her as one of the wonders of the world. My nervousness concerning my music and singing in front of hundreds of people after all these years was overruled by the anticipation of her presence.

She walked over to me and asked, "Are you nervous?" I answered, "Yes, a little." Small talk ensued, and she complimented me on my gown. In those few seconds, as I looked upon her grandness, I wondered how she achieved it. The special touch we refer to as "it" - she had "it"!

Immediately, this woman became my mentor. We discussed our relationship with God and promised to pray for each other. We discussed women in our position, how we got there and the pain it caused. She then reached into her bag of hidden wisdom and gave me the elements of being a great performer.

She explained how to overtake the stage, how to command the wood floors and the curtains that opened the stage for viewing to come alive to my personal attention. Her elegant, dramatic way lifted me into another realm that I didn't know existed. I had never seen a woman with such confidence. Or was it guts? Or style? I couldn't figure it out, and then it hit me. She knew *who she was.* She knew her *purpose* and developed it.

The Importance of a Woman

When it was time for me to walk out on that stage, I was ready. I had spent time with a master, someone who knew her value and had helped me to understand mine. And from that day to this, I have never been the same. I gathered my first element of understanding the importance of a woman. Element One: "*Know who you are and develop it.*"

The Curse of the Strong Woman *Karen Clark-Green*

1

Who Am I?

It is very hard to understand your purpose if you do not understand who you are. I have always heard the Lord say, "If the women get it together, the men will, too." This saying had puzzled me, but no more. Let's go back to the beginning and see why.

> And the Lord God planted a garden eastward in Eden; and there he put the man whom he had formed.
>
> And out of the ground made the Lord God to grow every tree that is pleasant to the sight, and good for food; the tree of life also in the midst of the garden, and the tree of knowledge of good and evil.
>
> And the Lord God took the man, and put him into the garden of Eden to dress it and to keep it.
>
> Genesis 2:8,9,15

The first thing God did was give the man a job. I always advise my single ladies that when handsome young men come inquiring to take them on a date, to respond very lovingly. Turn and look into their eyes and very sweetly ask, "Do you have a job?" It's scriptural!

And the Lord God commanded the man, saying, Of every tree of the garden thou mayest freely eat:

But of the tree of the knowledge of good and evil, thou shalt not eat of it: for in the day that thou eatest thereof thou shalt surely die.

Genesis 2:16,17

In these verses, God set boundaries. He made special mention of the tree of life and the tree of the knowledge of good and evil. God commanded Adam, **"Thou shalt not eat of it:,"** or thou shalt die. Adam should have been teaching Eve all that God had said. He should have had her at the tree of life partaking of it!

It is not so amazing that Eve was conversing with the Serpent. Remember Adam had named all of the animals and I believe that he could communicate with them. The Serpent had not yet been cursed and was in his original state. He walked upright on two legs and his countenance was like a brilliant light. So, it was not an usual thing that Eve would be in conversation with the Serpent.

The Hebrew translation for Serpent is, (nachash), it means: to hiss, to whisper, to shine! This creature spoke in a low lingering tone, but its body was full of light and attracted attention wherever it moved. So the creature, according to God's plan, had Eve's attention.

After God made everything, He said it was good or very good. (Genesis 1: 31) Now God introduces a new term.

And the Lord God said, It is not good that the man should be alone; I will make him an help meet for him.
Gen. 2:18

Whatever the man was or was not doing, God looked down at him and said, "This is not good!" I need to completely finish him, rearrange him, take what I have done and do it in another way that will be of more help to him.

And out of the ground the Lord God formed every beast of the field, and every fowl of the air; and brought them unto Adam to see what he would call them: and whatsoever Adam called every living creature, that was the name thereof.
Gen. 2:19

Adam named every living creature that God made. He lived and communicated with these animals for a period of time that we are not really familiar with. His understanding of each animal's characteristics is what allowed him to name them. However, God looked down on man and said something is not good.

Men seem to adjust more quickly than women. Adam was very happy and content in the state that he was in.

Adam had been absorbing the beauty and grandeur of the garden of Eden. He was happy tending the garden day after day, eternity after eternity. No one knows how long a period of time this was.

Men have a "conquer and move on" attitude. They put forth their best effort to get a woman or to accomplish a project. Once they have completed the task, they relax. They will place you (or whatever the accomplishment is) on a shelf, along with their other accomplishments. They think this will keep you while they move on to the next accomplishment.

Women are more restless, more easily bored. Men come home only to discover that the furniture has been moved around, the wife has started a new program and she has changed her hair, again! We are simply saying. "I AM BORED, AND I AM TRYING TO FIND SOMETHING TO DO." We do not want to be in the same place, doing the same thing over and over again!

In Genesis 1:26-28 God said:

.... **Let us make man in our image, after our likeness: and let them have dominion over the fish of the sea, and over the fowl of the air, and over the cattle, and over all the earth, and over every creeping thing that creepeth upon the earth.**

So, God created man in his own image, in the image of God, created he him; male and female created he them.

And God blessed them, and God said unto them, Be fruitful and multiply, and replenish the earth, and subdue it: and have dominion over the fish of the sea, and over the fowl of the air, and over every living thing that moveth upon the earth.

So, God created man, male and female. The visible part, "MAN" and the invisible part "WO-MAN." God then gave these instructions: **BE FRUITFUL AND MULTIPLY.**

When God looked down at man, he was content. You may still be in the mindset, "if woman hadn't eaten of the fruit, we would not be going through what we are going through today." You may be thinking that Eve's disobedience caught God off guard and so mankind fell.

We have no idea how long Adam and the woman were in the garden. We also do not have any idea of all the wonderful acts that they did together. Our limited thinking would lead us to envision the act of consummation as we understand consummation.

Once again, Adam became content. He adjusted quickly to this situation, while the woman was restless. That is why she was conversing with this magnificent creature, the serpent. He was crafty and exciting and had her full attention.

God said, **Be fruitful, and multiply, and replenish the earth.** This was not happening, so woman was trying to pacify herself. We would have started moving furniture. Woman was not content, the plan of God was not being fulfilled. She may not have fully understood what was suppose to happen, but she knew something was not being fulfilled and that they had to keep moving. Could Eve have been so desperate; to be fruitful, multiply and replenish the earth, that she was willing to risk death?

The word of God says that as the coming of the Lord Jesus Christ gets closer, knowledge (both natural and spiritual) will increase. There are treasures and gems in the Word of God that we should now be able to comprehend. We should know more than we knew a few years ago. We are also becoming more knowledgeable in understanding the English language. The church has no excuse for remaining illiterate.

The woman wanted to keep moving, because that is part of her purpose. You are probably still stuck at, **"Wives, submit yourselves unto your own Husbands..."** (Ephesians 5:22), which we are to do, but purpose must be understood before you can interpret and embrace vocation. The term, *man,* is used in a generic sense, which is amplified by the phrase, *male and female.* These are not the usual Hebrew words to indicate, *man, (ish) and woman (ishah).* The reason is, a completely unique relationship was to develop.

Woman did not fall. The word says that she was beguiled.

> **Now the serpent was more subtle than any beast of the field which the Lord God had made. And he said unto the woman, Yea, hath God said, Ye shall not eat of every tree of the garden?**
> *Genesis 3:1*

The serpent was created by God but used by Satan. The word says, **He was more subtle.** (Subtle in this sentence is rendered negative, which suggests "crafty.")

> **And the woman said unto the serpent, we may eat of the fruit of the trees of the garden:**
> **But of the fruit of the tree which is in the midst of the garden, God hath said, Ye shall not eat of it neither shall ye touch it, lest ye die.**
> **And the serpent said unto the woman, Ye shall not surely die.**
> **Genesis 3: 2-4**

I have my own interpretation of the account in the garden, it may have gone something like this:

The serpent was use to being in the garden with Adam and Eve. He had been there for some time. He spoke to Adam first, of course and then Eve. He appeared to be harmless and always stayed in his place when Adam was around. He was very in tune with the boredom and discontentment of the woman. He may have even appeared to be very helpful to her. His continued presence aroused the woman's curiosity until she began to trust him.

It is quite clear that the woman spent a lot of time with the serpent this is understood because God's word says that she was beguiled, which suggest that time was involved. Finally, the serpent is confident enough to make his move. He has learned all of her vulnerable spots and has won her confidence. "Hey, baby, you know that you are the most beautiful creature that God has made (even though he believes that he is). God has given you freedom to eat of all the fruit in the Garden."

The woman looks at him rather strangely. The serpent knows that he has struck a cord. "Ah, baby what's wrong, you can tell me, I've told you everything about me, you know that I am here for you (he gasped). Baby, did God say that you can't have all of this delicious fruit?"

Even though the serpent knew the answer, this lets us know that the serpent was amazed that God would restrict man's freedom of choice in the garden. Satan then centers in on the restriction, casting doubt on God's word. The serpent continues to use his craft. "Oh sweetheart," the serpent replied, "you won't die, not you!" "Do you know who you are? Without you, nothing is complete, that's your purpose. You did not understand, see God knew that in the day that you eat of this tree, you would know the difference between good and evil. Your eyes would be opened and you would be as God, which you deserve, with your fine self. He was not sure if you could handle it, that's all." (I have conversed with many snakes in my day and I know how they talk!)

The Word says that the woman was *beguiled,* which means that from her being in the presence of the serpent for a long period of time, he was able to trick or hoodwink her. *Beguiled* also means, "to please or persuade by the use of wiles or to charm." Woman didn't fully comprehend what was going on, however her spirit was saying, "lets get the ball rolling."

Woman who was blessed with influence, as all women are, used this gift to get Adam to partake of the fruit. As a result, mankind was brought to mortality, which gave us conditions for having children and for death. Woman knew as she talked with the serpent that something was happening. She was being tricked but she was also being pleased.

> **And when the woman saw that the tree was good for food, and that it was pleasant to the eyes, and a tree to be desired to make one wise, she took of the fruit there of, and did eat, and gave also unto her husband with her; and he did eat.**
> **Genesis 3:6**

Adam was in close proximity all the time, after all he introduced his wife to the serpent. The serpent was not intimidated by Adam. He didn't come as a low life, trying to get physical with Eve. He knew they were too intelligent for that. He was brilliant, suave, intellectual and gentle. The serpent knew that the woman's job called for great intelligence and that he couldn't just do anything with her.

A woman who falls for anything does not know who she is or what her purpose is. This is a sign that she has been pulled out of her place. When a woman gets to this point (because her self esteem has been shattered), she will fall for anything or anyone.

> **And the eyes of them both were opened, and they knew that they were naked; and they sewed fig leaves together, and made themselves aprons.**
>
> **And they heard the voice of the Lord God walking In the garden in the cool of the day: and Adam and his Wife hid themselves from the presence of the Lord God Amongst the trees of the garden.**
> **Genesis 3:7,8**

I once heard my pastor question what it must be like to hear the Voice of the Lord "walking". Keep in mind, man and woman were use to speaking and communing with God. His voice, presence and spirit were all one experience. Immediately a sense of guilt was felt and separation took place. The word *voice* probably translates better as "sound" (as it appears in Psalm 18:13; 29:3-9; Jeremiah 25:30, Ezekiel 1:24; and Joel 3:16) *walking* means, "traversing back and forth."

Adam and woman hid themselves from God's presence acknowledging that their intimate fellowship was broken. God always solicits a response from his creation. Immediately, He felt the separation and began asking questions.

Adam and the woman could no longer get the full experience of God's presence. They could only hear the sound of Him.

The Curse of the Strong Woman   *Karen Clark-Green*

2

THE WOMAN'S COVENANT

Authority was given to the man, but the greater influence was given to the woman. In Genesis 3:11-13, God questions Adam and Eve. Adam blamed the woman and God, since God was the one who gave Eve to him. Eve simply said, "I was beguiled, I was tricked, I was pleased by the serpent, and I did eat." However, she did not take full responsibility for the act either. The covenant God made with man was broken. But in Genesis 3:15,16, a new covenant was made:

> **And I will put enmity between thee and the woman, and between thy seed and her seed; it shall bruise thy head, and thou shalt bruise his heel.**

Unto the woman he said, I will greatly multiply thy sorrow and thy conception; in sorrow thou shalt bring forth children; and thy desire shall be to thy husband, and he shall rule over thee.

There are three truths in verse 15:
1. *Satan is the enemy of the human race,* explaining why God put enmity between the serpent and the woman. A war between woman and Satan is now in effect. The devil hates women. The word *enmity* denotes "enemy, asperity, animosity, maliciousness, hostility, discord and ill feelings."

There is a serious war going on between Satan and woman. Satan knows your purpose better than you do, so he is still out to deceive or beguile you because of *who you are.* Your influence is too great, and the world cannot function properly without you.

2. *God placed a spiritual barrier between Satan's domain and the woman's seed.*

3. *The representative seed of the woman (Christ) would deliver the death blow to Satan, but in doing so, Christ would be bruised.*

In verse 16, the word sorrow means "birth pangs." *Thy desire* is a physical desire strong enough to compensate for the pain of childbirth and natural desire to submit. In other words, if the woman was not under the desire of her husband, the devil would rule over her.

In Genesis 3:6, the first covenant was broken. Now, in Genesis 3:16, a new covenant was made with woman to give authority back to the man.

Under this covenant, the serpent was cursed (Genesis 3:14). God promised redemption through the seed of the woman (Genesis 3:15). Woman will experience multiplied sorrow or pain in childbearing (vs. 16). The ground was cursed (vs. 17,18). Sorrow, pain and physical death became part of the experience of life. Labor became burdensome (Genesis 3:19). Man even experienced sweat, which he had not known before the fall of man.

And Adam called his wife's name Eve; because she was the mother of all living.
Genesis 3:20

She was not called Eve prior to this time. Eve comes from the verb, "to live" or "mother of all living." She could not become the mother of all living until she became Eve. And, she could not become Eve until Adam knew her. The word 'knew' in this case means (intimate, intercourse, to know within). He named all of the living creatures because he spent time with them, he communicated with them and got to thoroughly know them. Now, he knew woman and his experience allowed him to name her.

The Curse of the Strong Woman   *Karen Clark-Green*

Part 2

The "Me" No One Knows

> For do I now persuade men, or God? or do I seek to please men? for if I yet pleased men, I should not be the servant of Christ.
> **Galatians 1:10**

Are you addicted to man's approval? Do you live your life pleasing everyone but yourself? Learning how to face rejection without being a people-pleaser will bring you into a reality of your self-worth.

Many people fail in life because of:

Hiding and protecting the real person inside.

Being afraid of making mistakes.

Letting others' opinions be an altering power in their lives.

Proverbs 23:7 says, **For as he thinketh in his heart, so is he.** Every person is born with natural gifts and talents that give them an element of greatness if they believe in themselves. I have read many books that have excited me about my potential. I learned that I can do some great things and I have all of these abilities that I never knew I had. Somehow I never got past this knowledge and I never experienced it. But I had to know who I was first, what I was capable of doing and what my personal purpose was. If you do not know who you are, you can't have a meaningful purpose.

Another problem for me was that all of the character-building in my life seemed to have come from the outside, not from within. So I was left without confidence in the natural gifts and talents. Yet, there was a great person inside that no one knew.

Element Two: *Believe in yourself and develop it.*

3

CREATED SPECIAL

We should now have a better understanding of what God had in mind when He created woman. Are we fulfilling our call as women?

Of all of God's creations, woman was created "special." Man was made from the dust of the ground, but not the woman. Woman was an important finishing product to help everything else that God had already made to function properly, so God did the first laser surgery and custom-designed woman. God touched man's heart by designing her. Then the Lord took her and gave her to Adam.

When Adam saw this creature - a creature he had not yet experienced - he was overwhelmed! Adam had grown accustomed to every kind of living creation that God had made. This creation was like him, yet so different.

God had created a wombed man or wo-man. A man with a womb or opening that held a cavity or space for enveloping and a place where something is generated. Certain hormones were put into this creation, unlike Adam's. These hormones gave wo-man some very attractive assets, which caused the emotions within Adam to react or come alive. She was called woman, because she was taken out of man.

Can you imagine the perfect woman? Can you imagine the gentleness, strength and confident beauty that she must have had? She knew why she was created and what her purpose was. She knew why she had hair on her head. Can you imagine what the perfect head of hair looked like?

She had the perfect body with the perfect walk. I'm sure her walk was a melody to Adam. He had seen camels, ants, lions and even chickens walk. But this walk was different. It was a walk that he had not yet experienced.

The time was now right for woman to speak her first words - a soft, gentle, nurturing sound that must have offered so much comfort that Adam's equilibrium was thrown off. Finally, he was able to touch this creature, experience her body and realize that all of this was to help make him more of a man - to complete him and help him to be who he was. Wow! No wonder God had to custom-design this important creature!

4

PEOPLE PLEASING

We all use excuses for not developing as God would have us do: "I'm too busy." "I have to take care of my family." "I'm too old." "I'm too young." "I didn't go to college." "I'm not good enough."

Our thoughts affect our personality and fuel us to be a success or a failure. We become who and what we think and feel. Many women mask their abilities and dreams. Many women hide their true identity. In fact, more women are people-pleasers than men.

People-pleasing keeps us depressed, stressed and angry. It also gives us a bad case of the blues. I have developed a teaching entitled, "Why Women Get the Blues," in which solutions to problems are offered.

The Curse of the Strong Woman   *Karen Clark-Green*

Women learned how to be people-pleasers through movies, television, newspapers, ads, the church and our families. We are told that our self-worth and value are tied to our success at nurturing or taking care of others. Most women will lay down their dreams in a minute to support their man's dream. The stronger a woman is, the quicker she will do it. The saying, "Behind every great man is a great woman," should be, "Behind every great man is a strong woman." Secretly tucked away in the inner being of some women is an unhappy, unfulfilled woman who has buried her dreams to fake happiness and make others' dreams come true.

In my studies, I have read about Maria Woodworth-Etter, who grew up in a small town in Ohio and was called to preach at the early age of thirteen. Maria was reared in a church denomination that did not believe in women ministers. Just because someone else does not believe in something that God is telling you to do does not take away the responsibility to be obedient to God and to the call on your life.

Maria did all the things that were expected of a young girl in the early 1900s. She married P. H. Woodworth because she was expected to get married.

Many women marry because they are "expected" to get married. Many women spend their lives seeking a mate to fulfill their purpose, because they don't understand that their relationship with God is a personal one. You don't necessarily need another person to fulfill the call of God on your life. Whether another person comes alongside or not, you are still responsible for the personal call that God has given you.

Maria's marriage was a disaster. (Women who are people-pleasers, who mask how unhappy they really are, often make wrong choices.) Maria and her husband had six children, which made Maria feel more and more responsible for the marriage. Deep in her heart, however, she lived in her dreams, desires and thoughts about the call to the ministry. She couldn't possibly answer that call, because people wouldn't accept it. She had traded her God-ordained purpose for the life she was now living.

Five of her six children died, and she became ill and was at the point of death. With each incident, the blues and the lack of self-worth got worse. Maria described a vision that she had from the Lord, which changed her life forever. He stood by her bed and spoke with her face to face. Jesus said, "You will tell the people of my glory."

When Maria decided to answer God's call, her obedience began to work a healing in her life. Wrong situations began to right themselves.

The results of her ministry are amazing. God did not change her husband or the people who were against her for being a minister. She didn't go to school for years of training. She looked inward to that being - her spirit man that God created from birth. This allowed her to start being real. Her second husband supported her in ministry. She was used to change Christian history and open the door for other women to minister.

When you become a people-pleaser, you give up your power. You believe that your sacrifice to others will please them enough for them to give something back to you. When you don't get it, you try to please them all the more. To get rid of the people-pleasing spirit, you must first admit that you are a people-pleaser.

1. Do you know what you stand for?
2. Is you life determined by others around you?
3. Do you find yourself doing things because you have been forced into doing them versus wanting to do them?
4. Have you put your dreams on a back burner and settled for a life that keeps you unfulfilled and unhappy?
5. Does your husband know your dreams and help to see them come to pass, or do you just support his dreams?
6. Is your life focused around everyone else's happiness before your own?

If you have answered "yes" to any of these questions, you are a people-pleaser.

Your success demands that you believe in yourself. Without this confidence, there will be no development. It is not too late for the "real you" to come forward and be a great success!

5

THE POWER OF INFLUENCE

Understanding your purpose as a woman should make you walk, talk and think differently. To understand that the earth cannot function properly without your presence should change your mind about who you are and your importance. The realization that you are the queen of the planet should help you to keep your crown in place!

Being created unique and special denotes an awesome responsibility. The greater *authority* was given to the man, but the greater *influence* was given to the woman. That influence is our power, and we have to be real for our power to work correctly. Our influence is always working, whether we realize it or not. We either influence someone to heaven or we influence them to hell. Every male, and really every person you come in contact with is being influenced by you.

God gave Adam authority, but the woman was given influence. Most women do not realize the responsibility of the influence they have. Eve, who had not yet been named, knew the power and responsibility of her influence over Adam. Satan also knew the power and responsibility of her influence over Adam. Why do you think Satan went to Eve and not directly to Adam? Satan was depending on Eve's influence to get Adam to do whatever Satan wanted him to do. The enemy will come to women with the motive of bringing down the man - the one with authority.

This principle works in the overtaking of a power. If you want to destroy a church, go to the babies, to the gossips, or to the rebellious ones. The devil never heads for the ones who are strong and spiritual. He always undermines authority in an attempt to get the authority.

As women we were created as helpmates. We will help or hinder according to the degree of righteousness and holiness that is coming from our lives.

Let's examine a few of the women in the Bible who used their influence for evil rather than good.

Bathsheba

> And it came to pass in an evening tide, that David arose from off his bed, and walked upon the roof of the king's house: and from the roof he saw a woman washing herself; and the woman was very beautiful to look upon.

> And David sent and inquired after the woman. And one said, Is not this Bathsheba, the daughter of Eliam, the wife of Uriah the Hittite?
>
> And David sent messengers, and took her; and she came in unto him, and he lay with her; for she was purified from her uncleanness: and she returned unto her house.
>
> 2 Samuel 11:2-4

When adultery was suggested to her, that's when Bathsheba should have used her influence and said, "No, thank you." Yes, David was the king and could have had any woman he wanted in the kingdom, but if Bathsheba would have resisted David, God would have vindicated her.

It is quite clear in the story of David and Bathsheba that Solomon had to be born. This indicates that God was going to give Bathsheba to David anyway! However, because Bathsheba did not use her influence for righteousness, it brought forth judgment. David's sin was punishable by death (Leviticus 20:10), although it was forgiven by God (Psalm 51). The sin of adultery had tragic consequences for David personally, for his own family and for his nation.

Delilah

Delilah's influence over Samson ultimately caused his death. What power that is to have your influence cause death! Let's look at this account in Judges 16:15-17:

And she said unto him, How canst thou say, I love thee, when thine heart is not with me? thou hast mocked me these three times, and hast not told me wherein thy great strength lieth.

And it came to pass, when she pressed him daily with her words, and urged him, so that his soul was vexed unto death;

That he told her all his heart, and said unto her, There hath not come a razor upon mine head; for I have been a Nazarite unto God from my mother's womb: if I be shaven, then my strength will go from me, and I shall become weak, and be like any other man.

Delilah used the method of nagging to get on Samson's nerves. Scripture says she nagged him daily, so that his soul was vexed unto death. Her influence worked for evil.

Chapters 2 and 5 of Proverbs warn of strange women with flattering words, because of the power of their influence.

Zipporah

A wife is to be a helpmate to her husband. Proverbs 31:11 says, **The heart of her husband doth safely trust in her, so that he shall have no need of spoil.**

The wife is to be a blessing, allowing the husband to remain at peace, because he knows he can trust her in all things.

God commanded Moses to circumcise his son. Zipporah did not understand and thought it was cruel. She did everything possible to keep Moses from obeying God. Moses listened to his wife, and as a result, almost lost his life. Zipporah's influence caused him to disobey God's will.

> And it came to pass by the way in the inn, that the Lord met him, and sought to kill him.
>
> Then Zipporah took a sharp stone, and cut off the foreskin of her son, and cast it at his feet, and said, Surely a bloody husband art thou to me.
>
> So he let him go: then she said, A bloody husband thou art, because of the circumcision.
>
> **Exodus 4:24-26**

Zipporah grabbed the knife because she knew she was the cause of Moses' disobedience. Moses' life was in jeopardy, because he was the authority figure.

Positive Influence

The biblical account of Abigail depicts a strong woman who is married to a weak man. She is an example of a woman using her influence for good.

First Samuel 25 portrays the choices this woman made. Abigail represents *wisdom*, while Nabal represents *the flesh* and King David represents *presumption*.

> And there was a man in Maon, whose possessions were in Carmel; and the man was very great, and he had three thousand sheep, and a thousand goats: and he was shearing his sheep in Carmel.
>
> Now the name of the man was Nabal; and the name of his wife Abigail: and she was a woman of good understanding, and of a beautiful countenance: but the man was churlish and evil in his doings; and he was of the house of Caleb.
> 1 Samuel 25:2, 3

This story takes place in Carmel, which is south of Hebron. Nabal is described as a great man of wealth and prestige. Nabal owned a lot of property and had many possessions, but his reputation as a leader was not good. People knew him as a drunk and churlish, which means prone to evil, thoughtless deeds against the poor. Nabal was a selfish man thinking only of himself and his possessions. His favorite words were *me, my* and *mine*.

Abigail was just the opposite in character. She is described as a woman of good understanding, which means she was wise. She had a beautiful countenance, which suggests an inner beauty that made her pleasant to look upon. As well as being beautiful she was blessed with natural assets. When God blesses you with natural assets, he will always allow something in your life to keep you humble. In Abigail's case, it was Nabal.

When Abigail entered a room, everyone stopped and looked to admire her beauty, charm and elegance. They were overwhelmed with her strength and grandeur. Nabal was loud, drunk and foolish. Abigail never thought more of herself than she ought. Nabal kept her humble and on her knees in prayer.

And David sent out ten young men, and David said unto the young men, Get you up to Carmel, and go to Nabal, and greet him in my name:

And thus shall ye say to him that liveth in prosperity, Peace be both to thee, and peace be to thine house, and peace be unto all that thou hast.

And now I have heard that thou hast shearers: now thy shepherds which were with us, we hurt them not, neither was there ought missing unto them, all the while they were in Carmel.

Ask thy young men, and they will show thee. Wherefore let the young men find favour in thine eyes: for we come in a good day: give, I pray thee, whatsoever cometh to thine hand unto thy servants, and to thy son David.

(1 Sam 25:5-8 KJV)

In war time, it was the custom of the day to protect the property of the person's land where you engaged in battle. It was now a time of peace, so David sent word to Nabal to ask for his just reward for protecting his property.

Shall I then take my bread, and my water, and my flesh that I have killed for my shearers, and give it unto men, whom I know not whence they be?
1 Samuel 25:11

Nabal refused to acknowledge David's request for compensation for guarding his flock, and he threw insults at David's men. David became very angry, and in his anger he decided to kill all of the men in Nabal's kingdom.

After hearing of the threat on their lives, one of the young men went to Abigail. How did he know to go to her? I believe her influence reflected her relationship with God. There must have been times in the past when similar situations were experienced and Abigail had proven her trustworthiness to seek and obey God. She did not have to call a fast or spend hours in prayer, because she was in constant communication with God.

Abigail quickly gathered practical items for David's reward. She knew she would have to go to him.

Since the woman is the glory of the man, why didn't Abigail reflect her husband? It seems as if some of the grandeur of Abigail would show in Nabal. As the story goes, people who looked on saw Nabal in his true state, and they saw Abigail in hers. A defection, a pulling away, a place left vacant or uncovered, or divorce, had already begun. This left Nabal exposed.

Abigail sent her servants before her with the reward and gifts for David. She sensed the politically tragic results of her wicked husband's foolish actions and used wisdom in not telling him of her plans. In this case, she was not in disobedience. I believe Abigail took the time to dress and prepare herself properly, understanding that she would be facing a king. She knew that all of her power as a woman was necessary for this task.

As she proceeded, she was apprehended by David and his men. In anger, David spoke of the good that he did in vain. He spoke of her foolish husband and how he repaid evil to David for good. He reiterated to Abigail that before morning, all of the men in their kingdom would be dead.

Immediately, she jumped down from her mule and laid prostrate at his feet. Her sensitivity to God's good intention for David caused her to submit herself to God's appointed ruler. She remembered her place as a woman, respect for those in authority and her God-given power of influence.

And fell at his feet, and said, Upon me, my lord, upon me let this iniquity be: and let thine handmaid, I pray thee, speak in thine audience, and hear the words of thine handmaid.

Let not my lord, I pray thee, regard this man of Belial, even Nabal: for as his name is, so is he; Nabal is his name, and folly is with him: but I thine handmaid saw not the young men of my lord, whom thou didst send.
1 Samuel 25:24, 25

Abigail interceded for Nabal and explained that he couldn't help himself, that he was as his name implied: "But no one came to me or I would have rewarded them." Immediately, her influence began to take effect. Her charm, quietness, beauty, respect, godliness and appreciation for David was witnessed by all the men. She asked David to receive the reward and gifts that she had brought. As he listened, Abigail began to prophesy to him, exclaiming that his life and the call to kingship upon his life was from God. She told him that he would be rewarded from the Lord since he did not shed blood that day. She influenced David towards good.

David began to thank God for her and that she had come to him. Abigail's manners and presence even kept David from hurting her. Now that David had cooled down, he realized that he was kept from avenging himself with his own hands. He sent Abigail back in peace, and told her that he gladly received her reward and gifts, and that he also accepted her. She replied, "When God blesses you and has dealt with you, remember me."

She returned home to find Nabal having a big party. He was drunk. She did not tell him all that had transpired. She was not being disobedient, but was using wisdom once again. The next day when Nabal was sober, Abigail explained all that she had done to save the kingdom. Nabal was a weak man, and his heart could not bear the embarrassment, so he suffered a stroke and died ten days later.

Abigail's influence kept David from taking vengeance into his own hands and bringing judgment on his house and his children. Possibly Nabal deserved what David was going to do to his kingdom, but David presumed that he should kill Nabal and his men. God never told David that killing Nabal was His will.

As the story ends, when David heard of Nabal's death, he sent word to Abigail to ask her hand in marriage. Abigail quickly accepted and prepared herself and five of her maidens to go to David.

David recognized that Abigail was a godly, wise woman. Influence used wisely saves lives, while influence used unwisely can cause death.

The Curse of the Strong Woman   *Karen Clark-Green*

6

THE MISSING CHILD

Story One

I watched and listened as comments were being made about my sister in the Lord: "She's backslidden." "She should be ashamed of herself." I thought, "Where is the compassion; the sensitivity? Couldn't they see through spiritual eyes instead of speaking with their judgmental mouths?"

My friend was a single parent with five children, all of whom she raised on her own. She was wed at the early age of nineteen, pregnant at twenty and divorced at twenty five. Whenever I saw her, I was amazed at her quiet beauty and femininity, yet there was an insecurity that I could not identify.

The Curse of the Strong Woman   Karen Clark-Green

She grew up with her children, trying to learn the vocation of motherhood through trial and error, like most of us. There was little time for anything but diapers, baby bottles, cleaning, etc. Her children grew to be preteens, then teenagers, ages 12, 13, 15, 16 and 17, all under one roof at one time, and four of them were girls!

We prayed and talked often. She told me of all her dreams, which seemed impossible. She was having relationship problems, because she didn't know how to have a relationship with a man. Being a happy child, developing into a healthy teen, into a young lady and then into a woman was an order she had missed.

Growing up in an environment with many siblings can sometimes leave you feeling lost. It was clear to me that she was probably labeled the black sheep in her family. Her mother also married young and never had the opportunity to develop into a responsible young woman. She was a child, bearing adult responsibilities and making adult decisions. My friend's example was her mother.

As I began to develop and change, I realized that there was this woman in me attempting to come forth. It was as if she was saying, "Ready or not, here I come!" I could see this happening to my friend. The woman in her was screaming, "Let me out." And the woman in her emerged.

Even though my friend was now thirty-eight, she began to behave like a nineteen year old. Why? Because that is where the real person stopped existing so she could deal with all the other vocations that were thrust upon her. She left the church choir, cut her hair into the style of the day, began to experiment with makeup and jewelry and changed her style of dress so we could not even recognize her. To others, her behavior was not acceptable, although it was normal behavior for a nineteen year old searching for her identity.

She got into two or three bad relationships looking for love and acceptance. She never learned how to deal with life's problems in a correct way, so whenever a problem came her way, she found comfort in a man. She didn't understand that she was seeking love and a father-daughter relationship that she never had. She was a grown woman who had been responsible to raise five children. One of her daughters had become pregnant, so she was also raising a granddaughter. In actuality, she was a little girl dressed in adult clothes, trying not to play the game of life.

When she turned forty, it got worse. To her it seemed as though life was passing her by and that she never had the opportunity to live. My friend was a spiritually wise woman, fighting her way out of a lack of never knowing who she was. She never had the opportunity to develop as a young child into a young lady, then into a healthy, mature woman.

This process took seven years. She is now remarried and has settled into womanhood. For the last two years, she has worked on the career that she thought she would never have. Now that she has grown up, it is becoming a reality. I expect this strong woman to become a congresswoman one day and tell her own story. She now understands her power as a woman and has learned to love herself first. And even more importantly, she has learned to trust God.

Story Two

Sandra, a quiet but spiritually powerful woman, was filled with potential in many areas of her life. Everyone she met knew she was somebody. You didn't know if you should approach her or not because of her regal presence. She was a very beautiful woman who seemed to draw attention everywhere she went. She was involved in many areas socially, politically, artistically and spiritually. I have seen her minister and have even had the opportunity to experience her anointing. I have wondered why the world doesn't know about this great woman. The call upon her life took a great amount of training and development, yet something seemed to constrain her.

Years went by and she was involved in many endeavors, but the breakthrough to excel to greatness just didn't seem to be there. The more we talked, I discovered the deep pain in her life. This amazed me, because she seemed to have it all together. She didn't complain and she never talked about people. In fact, she hated gossip and avoided people who were caught up in it. She was always kind and giving to people, but I never saw blessings equivalent to what she gave out.

Her love affair with God was obvious to everyone, although she was often misunderstood because of the in-depth revelations and insight that she had about the Word of God. It was as though she was ahead of her time, or in severe training for a secret mission.

As she continued to move with the cloud, more of her past was revealed to her and to me. We discussed the woman who emerges in a female at a certain age in life that cannot be restrained. As the woman in her came forth, she seemed to be in even more pain. While ministering to her, God began to speak of her self-protective mode and how she deadened herself to pain, in order to cope with the stress, strain and abuse in her life. Her childhood had been filled with physical and sexual abuse.

She had been molested as a young child by a cousin and had never told anyone because of fear and shame. Her father was an abusive, angry man, "but his behavior seemed to be normal when compared to other people I knew. All of our parents fought," she said. "We were disciplined with belts, extension cords, shoes, broom sticks and anything else they could get their hands on." She came from the "children should be seen and not heard" generation.

She felt guilty for not being able to protect her mother when her father would physically attack her. She felt anger and unforgiveness towards her mother for not protecting her from the molestation of her cousin. She felt hatred towards her father, because the only time he ever touched her was to discipline her. The deepest wound was that she was angry with God for allowing all of this to happen to her.

She realized the effects on her siblings, and had somehow thought that she had escaped. She knew that in Christ, old things had passed away and all things had become new, even though in her personality was embedded all of the hurt and anger that she had brought into the Kingdom with her.

She began to cry like a baby when she realized that sin was the culprit in her life - the sins of unforgiveness and of not trusting God. The child who had been beaten and molested hid so she wouldn't have to suffer pain. Her relationship with her father never gave her security in feeling good about herself, or in the ability to totally trust a male, including God. As a result, she always tried to earn love, because she thought she had to. She would allow cruel things to be said to her and instead of dealing with them, she would do the Christian thing, turning the other cheek until she couldn't bear the pain anymore. Then she would cut these people out of her life. The devil knew that if he could destroy the child in her, he would not have to worry about the adult.

Sandra was taken advantage of often, not realizing that the *hidden child in her was trying to "earn love."* She always went beyond the call of duty and was dependable. Her strength pushed her to excel. She developed programs to help people, taking charge of the most difficult task. *The child was trying to prove that she was strong.*

Sandra was self-sufficient, rarely calling on anyone to help her. If someone couldn't handle a job, or complete it, she would take on the responsibility with no one's help. She would give and give and give some more, ministering to individuals for hours at a time, but never received sufficient ministry for herself. The child was saying, *"God, Father, Mother, Husband, Friend, you didn't do a good job of protecting me, so I will protect myself."*

Sandra, the child, built a strong wall that fenced in Sandra, the adult. Now it was time to face the truth so the adult could emerge in fullness and power. God began to tear down the walls, because Sandra wanted a greater manifestation of God in her life. The unforgiveness towards God had to be released first.

The Lord began to show me how we deaden ourselves to pain. It may appear like something doesn't affect us. We give and give to a person, trying to earn acceptance or love, and finally come to a point where we cannot give any more.

We say, "You will never hurt me again." Or, "I'll never let you use me or talk to me like that again." In reality, we are deadening part of our heart so that it does not feel pain.

The trials that we go through develop compassion. They remind us of the pain that we suffered and make us relate to the pain of others so we can minister to them. The self-protective, deadening method that we use to keep from being hurt again keeps us from experiencing real passion in relationships, because we cannot risk feeling pain. Yet passion cannot be felt without pain. That missing child is hiding from pain and has also exempted herself from the joys of passion.

Through my pain, I have discovered wisdom, womanhood, new levels of spirituality, revelation and the true meaning of love.

For God so loved the world, that he gave his only begotten Son... (John 3:16). What a painful act, yet it reveals the essence of passion.

Now, the missing child in Sandra had been grafted in. That missing child had gifts and insight that are now prospering. When Satan heard of the coming of the Messiah he went looking for the child to destroy the adult. When Satan heard of the birth of Moses, he attempted to destroy the child to stop the adult. When Satan heard of your birth he attacked the child to stop the adult.

Now that you know his methods, you can release the missing child in you to grow up and feel the full benefits of love towards yourself, God and others. True passion requires feelings and feelings mean experiencing some pain to get the full context of any relationship.

The Curse of the Strong Woman   *Karen Clark-Green*

PART 3

THE STRONG WOMAN

A capable, intelligent, and virtuous woman who is he who can find her? She is far more precious than jewels and her value is far above rubies or pearls.

Proverbs 31:10 AMP

The summer of 1995 changed my life. It was the finality of a process that had been happening in me over the years. God had been teaching me how to access my future. He taught me that who I am is complete, and all I have to do is walk into my completed life.

I asked myself where that strong, bold woman that I used to be had gone? There was a time, if I decided to do something, nothing could stop me. If I needed money, I could obtain it.

If I needed strength, I could always muster it up. I realized that the real me, the one who God made, the one my mother named at birth, got lost in the midst of people-pleasing, compromise, defense-building and being off track. My new mindset taught me to arrange my life based on where I am going (my future) instead of where I have been (the past).

Once I became a wife and mother, I didn't know how to manage the original me. Two new vocations had been added to my life that I had not been trained for. So I tried to follow the examples that I had seen. All the TV moms that I grew up watching - Harriet Nelson, Mrs. Cleaver, you know the bunch - wore shirtwaist dresses, aprons, high heels and hair spray twenty-four hours a day! They spent most of their time in the kitchen, and never got their aprons dirty. They waited on everyone hand and foot, and always looked as if they had just left the beauty parlor.

Being an artist, I have always had the drive to excel at what I do, so I put "my all" into it. The real me took a back seat to the roles that I was now attempting to portray. It seemed right, because I had many examples of women before me who did the same thing.

Element Three: *Your life is complete!*

7

CHANGE YOUR MIND

The changes that were happening to me began to expedite themselves and my faith in what God had shown me deepened.

For years my prayer was, "Put me back where I got off track." Time was now in route to kiss destiny! I was on the road back to my purpose! God had a particular plan designed exclusively for me. The power was in God's thought, and I am that thought in the flesh.

Proverbs 23:7 says, **For as he thinketh in his heart, so is he...** Thinking is power, not knowledge. Your thoughts equal you. What you think of yourself is who you will become. If you think less, you will become less. If you think more, you will become more.

I have the understanding of my basic, general purpose for existing and of the power of my influence. I am learning my value as a woman, the power that I possess and how to be responsible with it.

The Curse of the Strong Woman   *Karen Clark-Green*

A colleague once asked me, "What is the fun of being a woman?" The question shocked me. I knew I didn't have an answer, because it hadn't been fun. I just didn't know how to admit it.

In my heart, I desired to be free - free not only in spirit, but free to be who I really am. I felt as if my purpose and my power were coming into focus and that destiny was not far off. I realized that change had to take place within me for me to become the real me. Some powerful force had reshaped me mentally, physically, emotionally and spiritually. I had done feats out of God's will, and I was made to believe that the person I had become was me.

God only has one will. Perhaps you have been taught that He has two wills: a permissive will and a perfect will. Now that you are learning the truth, you must change your mind to proceed.

The unique plan that God has for you will bring you to the realization of your good points as well as your bad points. Some of the mistakes you thought you made weren't mistakes. They were in God's plan. No matter how painful, the mistakes made you face some hard facts. All of us have made the foolish statement, "If I had it to do over again, I would not make that same mistake again!" Yes, you would! You would do everything just like you did it the first time, because that is who you were at that time and place.

The new person that I was becoming perceived things differently. The truth had been confused with lies and strength had been confused with weakness. Yet there was a familiarity to this new person that I could not comprehend. The more I learned of my power and purpose as a woman, I felt closer to God. I was moving forward, yet heading back to my original purpose - to the original thought that God had of me.

Everything about me was beginning to change. Things must change to prepare for a new thing.

I began to understand that change begins with honesty, and I had to be honest with myself. I had to face reality. I had to tear down my alternate world to enter the real world. The weight of living a lie is burdensome. You may not yet see that not facing the truth is living a lie, but keep on reading!

Do you understand the emotional strain it takes to be involved in a cover-up? If you are not feeling well because of the cover-up, and someone asks you what is wrong, you have to lie. You cannot tell them the truth. Honesty takes away the need to live a lie. The truth alone will make you free. Honesty will make you face the reality of your life and put it in proper perspective so you can see things the way they really are.

If you want the ultimate out of life, you must be willing to change and keep changing or growing. If you are not willing to change, you have reached your maximum in life and nothing else awaits you.

The Curse of the Strong Woman *Karen Clark-Green*

8

THE NEXT LEVEL

My pastor, Bishop Norman L. Wagner, had begun to teach on living on the next level and how to access the living principles of not being bound by the earth. This was great revelation to me.

I would go to Bible study and sit in awe of the limitless knowledge that God has for all who want to partake. God will give you as much as you can stand. This level of teaching, combined with my power and influence, put me on the stairway to the next level. I listened to my pastor proclaim, "Go to the next level." I wanted to scream, "I am going! I am going!"

I have learned through the years with the Lord that when speaking of knowledge, growth, blessings, or anointing, you are asking for tests and trials. These tests and trials will develop circumstances to force you to the next step. To take the next step, the first step must be completed. I wanted to go to the next level, but I thought to myself, "What will it cost me?" Am I suggesting that there is a price to serve the Lord? Yes, I am. Salvation is free, but an anointing and deeper knowledge of God will cost you something.

I wanted the fullness of life, which I knew only comes through the Lord Jesus Christ. Living requires dying. The death of one thing means the beginning of a new thing. Most of us believe that endings or death are always negative. If you have just received notice that your job has been terminated, rejoice! It means that phase of your life has ended, and a whole new life-altering experience awaits you. If you've just lost your position in the church or on a board, rejoice! A new position awaits you.

You are probably thinking, "Sister Karen, the experience that I had was negative. I was hurt, embarrassed and I felt destroyed." Or, "I don't have a job. How will I live? How will I feed my children?" You will live by faith and trust God that these experiences of life are accomplishing the growth necessary so you can graduate to the next level.

The ax must be put to the root of the tree to cut the whole thing down. Don't leave any of it to sprout up again. Maybe I should say, "Don't look back!"

Women like to reminisce and have keepsakes. Until a door is completely closed, new doors cannot open. You cannot hold on to the pain and unforgiveness of an experience, but you must make a choice to let go. When you don't let go, you don't move. All the root was not taken up, so that experience has you tangled up in it.

In the meantime, because you are in limbo, seasons pass with your blessings. You are screaming, "God, how could you do this to me?" You probably had to collect unemployment or go on welfare because your income was affected. You are still talking about the old job and how the people at the church or in some organization hurt you.

Your spirit knew change was taking place and that you were in the process of moving up a step. Your heart was saying, "This is frightening, uncomfortable and is making me feel out of control. If my situation had not changed, I would not feel like this. If I was back in what God just kicked me out of, I would feel safe."

You must understand, the future holds things that you are not familiar with in your present situation. There is no history in your past indicating where you are going in your future. You are on strange territory and you are frightened.

This past year was difficult for me, yet it brought maximum growth. We experienced bankruptcy. We lost our home. I had two pianos, now I have none. Other items that were dear to me are gone. I was worried about my children and the effect all of this would have on them. I didn't know where the money we needed would come from. I fought to not lose my mind.

I made the decision to give up the building where I held classes for our Performing Arts Centre. This only affected the instructional division. I must admit, however, it really was a relief in some ways for me. I was not able to perform a lot because I was tied to the functioning of the Centre.

In the midst of all this, new ventures were developing. Something within me was changing, along with the changes that were occurring in my life. I was entering unfamiliar territory, going some place I had never been before. The year was a time of severe depression and anxiety.

Even though I was at the apex of my pain, God was making a new person out of me and He was developing a new, joy within me. I realized I was getting a deeper insight into the things of God and a deeper relationship with Him that was priceless.

Endings are painful. We have to let go of something we have held, nurtured, or touched and realize that it is over. This is not easy to deal with. Unless you deal with it, however, you will stop progress. You have to let go, forget how things used to be and walk on in the newness of life.

Often, I would get together with my friend, Regina, another minister who was also in the midst of writing a book. We would pray together and seek God. We would discuss the price it was taking to write a book. We knew we were on the next level. In the midst of our desperate search for comfort from God, I jokingly described to her what I saw as a road map to the next level.

I made her envision this beautiful brochure that described a wonderful spiritual oasis, with unbelievable knowledge and a great anointing, and a road map of how to get there. The directions are:

Go to the road where all the beautiful trees are. You will know because the scenery is so overwhelming. When you get to the beautiful castle at the top of the hill, where the rose garden is and the lake where the swans are, make a sharp right turn onto *Sadness Lane*. It will be dark there, but just keep going.

When you come to a fork in the road, take the road to the left. For some reason it always rains on this road. It will take you to *Grief Street*. I hope you have a spare tire, many people have flat tires on this road. Follow the bend in the road and look for *Sorrow Avenue,* then take a left. This is a winding road, and it will make you think you are going in circles if you don't keep your mind focused. You will come to a clearing at the top of the mountain. It is always so peaceful there. You will see a sign that says, *"Welcome to the Valley of the Shadow of Death."* When you see this sign, get excited! You are almost there. It is on the other side of the valley. Everyone is *not* willing to go. Please understand, yes, it will cost you something. It will cost you everything that you have and ever thought of having. It will cost you your comfort, your agenda, your career and your life. You really do have to lose your life to find it. You must die daily to the inclination to live a lie. Our suffering on the cross is to lose ourselves and take up His cross in the reality of who we really are.

Dreams and visions come to pass on this next level, not to mention the blessings. So, come on, take the first step!

The Curse of the Strong Woman   *Karen Clark-Green*

9

THE VIRTUOUS WOMAN - WHO CAN FIND ONE?

When we speak of the ideal woman, is the word *strong* ever used? What do we mean by *strong*? Are we speaking of physical strength, or strength of character? Are we speaking of the ability to run a household, a business, or a corporation? Is the power of strength in our tongue or in our hearts. Do we believe that the woman who is forceful, loud, domineering and bossy to be the strong one? Do we have any idea what a "strong" woman is?

I have heard teaching on Proverbs 31 many times. All of us who are seeking to be the woman God wants us to be have tried everything possible to obtain this goal. Proverbs 31 is spoken by King Lemuel's mother. None of us know who King Lemuel is. We only know that he was a son who received wise teachings from his mother. *Lemuel* means, "devoted to God."

The book of Proverbs begins with the command to trust and reverence the Lord and ends with a picture of a woman who fulfills this command. She begins by explaining that the wrong woman would destroy him, that women have been used to destroy kings and kingdoms.

Proverbs 31:3 says, **"Give not thy strength unto women, nor thy ways to that which destroyeth kings."** Lemuel's mother goes on to explain that wine and whiskey are not for kings, because it can affect the fulfillment of their duties and their decision-making. It seems as though Lemuel's mother is giving him the secrets of being a successful man, a successful king and how to have a successful life.

Proverbs 31:10 says, **"Who can find a virtuous woman** (which translates "wife")? **for her price is far above rubies."** In other words, if you find a truly good wife (there is a difference in finding a wife and finding a woman), she is worth more than any precious stones. Proverbs 18:22 supports this verse: **"Whoso findeth a wife findeth a good thing, and obtaineth favour of the Lord."**

This verse says that finding the right wife will give the husband favor with God. If that is so, it seems to me that a man who finds a wrong woman, one that God does not consider a wife, will not receive God's favor.

Proverbs 31:11,12 says, **"The heart of her husband doth safely trust in her, so that he shall have no need of spoil. She will do him good and not evil all the days of her life."**

This kind of woman can be trusted by her husband in all things. She will tend to him and satisfy his needs. She will in no way be a hindrance to him, but will help him all of her life. She will be faithful to him.

Even when she is old and all she can do is speak, she will have words of wisdom to give him. This seems to be a special power that women have. In this case, I see power and strength being synonymous.

Proverbs 31:13-19 says:

> **She seeketh wool, and flax, and worketh willingly with her hands.**
> **She is like the merchants' ships; she bringeth her food from afar.**
> **She riseth also while it is yet night, and giveth meat to her household, and a portion to her maidens.**
> **She considereth a field, and buyeth it: with the fruit of her hands she planteth a vineyard.**
> **She girdeth her loins with strength, and strengtheneth her arms.**
> **She perceiveth that her merchandise is good: her candle goeth not out by night.**
> **She layeth her hands to the spindle, and her hands hold the distaff.**

Many people have the mistaken idea that the woman described here is totally domestic and servile (humbly submissive). The woman I am reading about is a busy, energetic woman, with outstanding abilities. This woman craves the best for her family. Verse 16 says she goes out to inspect a field and makes the decision to buy it! (Yes, ladies, she made that decision on her own.) Verse 17 states that she is not only energetic, but she strengthens her arms. In other words, she works to be physically fit.

The Curse of the Strong Woman — Karen Clark-Green

Proverbs 31:20-31 says:

She stretcheth out her hand to the poor; yea, she reacheth forth her hands to the needy.

She is not afraid of the snow for her household: for all her household are clothed with scarlet.

She maketh herself coverings of tapestry; her clothing is silk and purple.

Her husband is known in the gates, when he sitteth among the elders of the land.

She maketh fine linen, and selleth it; and delivereth girdles unto the merchant.

Strength and honour are her clothing; and she shall rejoice in time to come.

She openeth her mouth with wisdom; and in her tongue is the law of kindness.

She looketh well to the ways of her household, and eateth not the bread of idleness.

Her children arise up, and call her blessed; her husband also, and he praiseth her.

Many daughters have done virtuously, but thou excellest them all.

Favour is deceitful, and beauty is vain: but a woman that feareth the Lord, she shall be praised.

Give her of the fruit of her hands; and let her own works praise her in the gates.

This is a woman who takes pride in taking care of the household. She also takes pride in her appearance. Some women believe their call in life is to go shopping or that their ministry is to look good. We are supposed to look good but if these other character qualities are not present in our womanhood, we can shop until we drop! All we are doing is putting our husbands in debt. To top it off, there is not a outfit made that will cover your lack as a woman!

A woman's strength and dignity do not come from her achievements. They come from her reverence for God. This woman is made from the inside out instead of from the outside in. In today's society, physical appearance is a major deciding factor in attractions. This is fine in getting someone's attention, but if this is all there is, then you are setting yourself up for more misery than you can handle. There is a beauty of character that can anoint our physical presence to overwhelm others so they can comprehend our true beauty.

The virtuous woman is described as the best of all women, the cream of the crop, a woman of strong character great wisdom, many skills and compassion.

Verse 26 states that even her manner of speaking offers wisdom, love and kindness. All of us know women (maybe you are one of them) with overwhelming personalities and commanding ways of expression. We have always looked at these characteristics as strength. The domineering woman who takes over and is loud, forceful and rough tries to convince you that she is strong through manipulative measures. The word *strong* does mean force. It also means "having power that is not easily broken; firm, effective and earnest." *Strength* is having power, support, vigor, intensity, to be relied upon, or to have faith in. Many women respond: "Well that's my personality. God made me this way. My mother was like this, and my grandmother, too." It is true that you had to learn it somewhere.

I'm not saying this kind of personality is wrong. But I am saying that scripture helps us to understand the attributes of a godly woman. Scripture also warns of strange women with flattering tongues. Some of the quiet, never-bother-anybody women, can be deadly. We have simply taken what we believe to be strength and have not realized that it is weakness -

weakness that comes from the need to protect ourselves from pain.

First Peter 3:4 says, **"But let it be the hidden man of the heart, in that which is not corruptible, even the ornament of a meek and quiet spirit, which is in the sight of God of great price."** This verse refers to being beautiful *inside*.

We should spend as much time developing our character as we spend on our appearance. An ornament is something that you put on. So we have to be willing to put on a meek and quiet spirit, which according to Scripture, is precious in the sight of the Lord. We think of meek and quiet as weak, but my interpretation of a meek and quiet spirit is *strength of character and wisdom,* not shallow, loud, or cheap, but tranquil and under control, and that is not weak!

The virtuous woman is a guide or an example for other women to line up with. No one possesses all of these characteristics, but we should strive to. The virtuous woman is well provided for and secure, which helps her to be the woman she is to be.

10

THE LION AND THE LAMB

Women used to look for a mate who would support them and take care of them. This enhanced their feminine behavior. It made a relationship simple - you stay in your role, and I will stay in mine. This was an acceptable way of life.

The traditional roles no longer exist. When I was growing up, a girl would never call a boy first or make the first move. Not so today. Success used to be tied to the man you married, but today everything a man can provide for his wife she most likely can provide for herself. For some, it is not a choice but a necessity that they become the head of the house. These women are forced into the masculine role. It is very hard to assume male responsibilities and keep your femininity intact, without proper understanding of balancing the lion and the lamb.

The Women's Liberation Movement of the 60's and 70's assured women that they were equal to men, could do anything a man could do and could have anything a man could have. They told us we could do it all, but they did not tell us how to do it or the side effects that were guaranteed to develop.

It amazed me that a woman's role still had to be filled, even though she might take on two or three more roles as a wife, mother and managing the home.

When the head of the house comes home from a hard day's work, he likes to have his dinner cooked, take a bath, sit down, relax and have his feet rubbed. When you come home from work, you may get a chance to change your clothes, but you still have to straighten up the house, wash clothes, cook dinner and you still may have to rub his feet!

If there are children, the bulk of the responsibility for the care still falls on you. The general understanding is, *the woman should resolve it*. Today's society says, *the woman can do it all*. This has her vacillating between the male and female roles.

A woman has a natural, God-given need to be protected. It is part of her female power. When a man sacrificially submits himself to God to receive the understanding of how to nourish and cherish his wife, he is meeting her deepest marital need to be secure.

But when a woman carries the burden for the security of herself and/or her family, she must become the lion (the protector). To approach the mother of a lion cub or bear cub after you have mishandled or frightened her children can be very dangerous. Do you want to see a gentle, docile Christian woman (a lamb) turn into a raging lion? Then mess with her children, and the protector (the Lion) will come forth. She must come out of her natural state (as that of a lamb) to emotionally, physically and spiritually deal with the challenge.

A man's deepest marital need is to be honored and respected. Neither male nor female can provide for their own needs completely. Proverbs 28:26 says, **"He that trusteth in his own heart is a fool."** *Your deepest needs cannot be met without God.*

Spiritual people will always pull out Scripture that says, *"Our trust is in God, not man."* Even though most of the women I know walk around quoting Scripture, they are still praying for someone to meet their needs. They know that God can hold and caress them, but they still crave real arms made of flesh.

Being in God's will, will help you find someone with whom you can experience godly love. The secret is trusting and believing God to do it. We will be disappointed if our trust for security and happiness is only in a person.

Jeremiah 17:5 says, ...**Cursed be the man that trusteth in man, and maketh flesh his arm...**

As I mentioned earlier, a woman's basic need is security. If we understand this priority and put God first, before any man, it will keep us from being devastated during times of tests and trials when security may not be present.

Everywhere we look today, women are lions in business and lions seeking power, money and prestige. They are seeking respect instead of seeking to be cherished. They are seeking the deepest need of the male (the lion) instead of the deepest need of the female (the lamb). What has happened to make everything so topsy-turvy? It is bad relationships, unforgiveness, sins of the fathers passed on through the bloodline, wrong mother-son relationships, wrong father-daughter relationships. Although this will have an effect, I believe it is because of *not seeking God and trusting Him first.*

We have been learning about the limitless power we have as women in our God-given roles. We need to understand what makes us tick. How do you expect your significant other to understand you if you don't understand yourself? There will be times in life when you must call the lion forth, but you have to know when.

A woman's four basic needs are: security, affection, open communication and leadership.

Security - To be secure doesn't apply to finances alone. This basic need for every female, single or married, is to feel safe and well provided for in every area. A wife desires security from a husband who is in submission to God and who will receive knowledge of how to provide protection and provision. A woman can recognize or sense when a man's heart is committed to her care and well-being. A wife's well-being will be dependent on her husband. This will affect her spiritual growth and her peace of mind.

Story One

A husband and wife, along with their children, went camping one weekend. The wife has never been camping before, because she is afraid of roughing it. She knows that she will be exposed to the elements and isn't sure of being properly protected.

When they arrive at the camp site, she knows that she has to be able to function in her duties of preparing the meals and making the inside of the tent comfortable. Her husband unloads the gear and begins to very carefully put the tents up, making sure every piece is in place and secured.

When he is finished, she stands back and looks. These are nice tents, every pole and rope in place. It looks as if the tents can stand the strongest wind. She gives a sigh of relief and feels secure (or loved) enough for her and the children to stay in the tent.

Now, it is time to build a fire. She has never cooked on an open fire. What if he gets the wrong kind of firewood? Will the fire get out of control and burn her? What if the fire is not made right and goes out in the midst of her cooking? The husband takes his time and carefully finds the right firewood so she will not have to fear the fire going out.

The fire is high and perfect, so she feels secure enough (or loved enough) to start the meal. What if he does not think she can cook a good meal on an open fire? He assures her that he trusts her abilities.

Finally, it is time to go to bed. "Do we have the proper bedding? Will the children be warm enough?" The husband pulls out the sleeping bags and kerosene lamp and properly rekindles the fire outside the tent to keep all stray animals away and secures the tent from wind and cold.

The family climbs into their sleeping bags, and the wife feels secure and trusts in her husband's ability to take care of her. She feels so secure that now she wants to show her gratitude to her loving husband. She respects him for providing properly for her and the children, and now the lambs wants to reward him.

Story Two

A husband wants to surprise his wife, so he buys her a new home. He takes her to the neighborhood, and inwardly she thinks, "This is out of my children's school district. How will they get to school?"

The house looks secure from the outside, but the yard is unkempt. Two windows are broken and the steps are cracked. She is afraid that her children might get hurt. She doesn't feel secure. As she goes inside, she sees all of the repairs that are needed and wonders if they would ever get done. She thinks of all the repairs at her old house and how she has had to take care of most of them. She is working on a special project that might make enough money to help with the repairs on the house. The husband, however, told her that he felt she was wasting her time and that he would do his job and provide the money for the family. This made her feel insecure in her abilities.

They moved in and after a week, a bad storm caused the basement to flood. The gas bill hadn't been paid, so in the midst of her cooking, the gas was cut off. Regardless how many blankets were piled on the children, they were still cold. That night as they went to bed, she moved into her protector mode (the lion), wondering and worrying how they would take care of the children.

As she looked at her husband, in a deep sleep beside her, she felt insecure, wondering if he could take care of her and the children, and if he would ever believe in her abilities.

When her husband awakened and turned affectionately to his wife, she could not reward him. In fact, it took everything she had not to pack her bags, grab her children and leave. She was not free to be the woman she was created to be.

Do You Understand?

To get your man to understand this, you may have to relate it in an analogy to his employer. If his employer is a cheat and holds back funds, the employees won't trust him. If the employer says, "We are losing money I am going to have to cut your salaries back and lay some of you off," the security in the job is gone, and it will affect performance. On the other hand, if the boss is always making improvements, giving holiday or unexpected bonuses and is of good reputation, you will feel safe and secure and will give your best on the job.

Not only do women need to be told that they are safe with their man, but they must also be shown. This is the only way the man will receive the full benefit of the female power (the lamb), whether he is the husband, pastor, father, or friend.

Affection - Affection and sex are *not* the same thing. Women must understand that men are turned on by sight, any time and any place. On the contrary, women are turned on by affection and intimate, non-sexual quality times together.

What attracted your man to you in the first place may have been your sex appeal. It is up to you to show that you have more to offer. This will cause him to want to commit to you and cherish you. Non-sexual affection makes you feel secure as a woman. A man must learn this key. If a woman is made to feel that her value is in sex alone, her femininity will shut down. She will move into a "want to please mode" and have sex even when it causes her emotional pain. At these times, a woman must be assertive and let her self protecting mode (the lion) take over.

A woman must communicate what she is feeling to receive the full benefits of being a woman. Pleasing the one you love is a good thing. It is when it causes you harm that it is not good.

Many women feel guilty or inadequate because they have trouble responding to their instant sex partner. Yet they are never aroused, because women respond differently. If a woman feels this way, she is not safe in your care. In order for her to overcome this problem and prevent emotional destruction, she must force herself to let her man know that she is not satisfied and teach him how to be affectionate.

Quality non-sexual affection is a "must" to nurture the lamb in a relationship, which will keep her walking, talking, thinking and reacting like a woman (the lamb).

Open Communication - When sensitive talk and attentive listening are happening in a relationship, it will bloom. Otherwise, it will deteriorate. A woman's emotions and influence are developed through communication. This kind of communication makes a woman feel special and of value and builds intimacy. If a woman does not feel valued, she will feel used. This will affect her self-worth and her ability to communicate.

Unsettled issues in a woman's past will affect her present state. She may need to verbalize these issues to be healed. She will do this only if she feels safe with the person she is communicating with, whether it is male or female.

Women have an innate desire to nurture, take care of, or to be concerned with. If loved ones around us are not feeling good, we often feel it is our fault unless we are told otherwise. Male and female relationships, where the man does not have open communication with the female, will make the female feel as if she has done something wrong, because in her presence, the male is not at peace. It is deadly to a woman, as well as to a man, to tell him/her something is wrong without explaining what it is. She will conjure up all kinds of things in her mind that she might have done, which will destroy her power and cause her to feel as though her influence is inadequate.

Leadership - A woman is made to follow. I don't care how strong she appears or what corporation she heads up, there are times she will want to put the lion to rest and let her natural state, (the lamb) come forth. Without effective leadership, she cannot do this.

Single women in a church, where leadership is strong and effective, will be a strength to that particular body. These churches will have less women involved in gossip and more women seeking their spiritual place for that body and in the Body of Christ.

A husband in his place, being a good leader, contributes to his wife's power. This in turn compliments him in a correct way and helps to build his manhood.

A corporation or business with strong leadership always has strong effective women who are building a reputation for that corporation, business or leader. Bad leaders will arouse the lion in the female, and she will take over. However, she will leave a great deal of her femininity behind in order to do it.

The lion in women is not all bad, but it will emerge negatively when they feel threatened, unsafe or not cherished. The positive lion takes care of business, gives rewards and protects. Only God can give us balance in this area.

I have always said that, "the mark of a wise women is to know when to shut up!" You only know this when the lamb is in control. A woman in rebellion will move into a leadership, protective role, twenty four hours a day. She will nag, be bossy and forceful, or any other way she needs to be to get the job done. What she doesn't realize is, if she is doing the man's job, he won't. He will say, "if you are man enough to do it, go right ahead." The truth is, she is not feeling good because she is not feeling cherished. She is simply saying, "make me feel safe, talk to me, lead me and I will be the most loving woman you have ever dreamed of."

11
WHAT YOU SEE IS WHAT YOU GET

God created men and women differently, but basically, we want the same things. Our expectations are different. Men want their wives to be there for them, to nurture them and be a support in the full context of a "help mate."

Women expect their men to be best friends and someone with whom they can share their deepest secrets. They expect them to take care of them and protect them as if they are their most valuable possession. So women complain that their men don't communicate, because women want to *hear* what their men feel. And men complain because they want *to see* what their women feel.

The emotional intimacy requirements of men and women may be the same, but they are expressed differently. It will greatly help, not only if we understand those differences, but we must translate our language of expression to our loved ones.

Most women are still looking for their knight in shining armor to come and rescue them and take them off into marital bliss. If you are waiting to be rescued, you are not spending time investing in your value. I guarantee you, the knight you are waiting for will never show up, and if he does, you will not be woman enough for him.

Marriage must be worked at. Practice in your marriage just like you do in your job or career. I try to remind my single sisters who are still waiting on that knight in shining armor, when he shows up, just remember, someone has to clean up after his horse, and it probably will be you!

Women have a hard time accepting men for who and what they are. They may see that he is not good for them, but they actually believe they can change him. The reality is that a couple with those kinds of expectations will not be able to meet each other's basic needs in the manner that has been anticipated. The courtship time is a time of learning about each other and understanding, *what you see is what you get!*

Strong women are not out to change a man but to compliment and complete him so they themselves can be complete. They understand the importance of being the right rib. Unless you are the right rib, you will never fit. No matter how you twist, turn, push, or bend, no matter if it takes fifteen years or five months to realize it, *only the right rib will fit!*

So what is a "strong woman"? A strong woman is one who knows who she is and who loves herself. She understands her femininity and masculinity (the lion and the lamb) and how to balance them. It is impossible for a woman to be 100 percent feminine all the time. The lamb is 80 percent of what makes the woman attractive. But without the lion, you probably won't get anything done. Career women must exert their lion or they will definitely be taken advantage of. So you must learn how to balance the lion and the lamb in you.

You must know the needs of your mate as a man. He, like you, has a lion and a lamb within him. Most men are 80 percent lion and 20 percent lamb. Keep in mind, some men are 60 percent lion and 40 percent lamb. Sometimes you can even see their femininity. This doesn't mean they are homosexual. It means they are just as sensitive as you are, possibly even more so.

As men and women get older, the balance changes. Men acquire more lamb and women acquire more lion. Some men over forty, especially career men who are corporate leaders and in authority positions, like to put their lion away when they come home. They have been the protector, giver, aggressor all day at work. Now, they want you to pursue them, be the aggressor and give them a chance to unwind. I am *not* talking about a weak man - one who is not taking care of responsibilities or who is not giving - yet this man wants you to lead and do everything. He is not a lion or a lamb. Instead, he is a narcissistic taker!

The lion (masculine) is a natural giver, protector and cherisher. He likes to solve problems and take on challenges. In fact, the bigger the challenge, the better he likes it. The lamb (feminine) is a receiver. Women have always thought they were the givers, and that doing everything for their men would cause him to love them more. This kind of behavior only weakens him, because it puts the woman in control.

Your mate wants to be appreciated, accepted and trusted. I am not talking about respect at this point, which is a masculine quality. Both men and women need to be respected.

Appreciation - Appreciation lets him know that everything about him, negative and positive, is valued.

Acceptance - Acceptance tells a man that he is fine the way he is and that you are not expecting him to change. Women who want to change their men never accepted who they were in the first place.

Trust - Trust tells a man that he is a good person. It tells him that he is honest, reliable and sincere. The wife believes she can confide her deepest secrets in him. Trust from the female can deepen the relationship, while mistrust or lack of trust builds walls and eventually causes the man to withdraw. Most women do not understand men's emotional needs, and that withdrawing a trust they were once given will cause emotional pain to the male.

Remember, the man wants to be your protector. How can he protect you if you don't trust him? How can God provide for you if you don't trust Him to do it?

Women in the church have looked at spirituality as an attractive masculine quality, that they need to master in or to be powerful. Not true, that is not where your power lies! Many women in the church make themselves unattractive by the fake, loud, hard covering they put on, trying to appear spiritual. They take off their makeup and jewelry. Next they stop wearing feminine clothes and put away their negligee and lingerie. Out of nowhere the non-feminine apparel shows up, thinking they are now somehow closer to God. This is a form of powerlessness, which makes you less potent as a spiritual woman.

While ministering at a convention, a pastor came to me after hearing the teaching on couples. He began to share with me how his wife used to dress and care for herself before she was saved. "She accused me of not wanting to be seen with her," he said. He exclaimed that he loved his wife, he just wished that she would fix herself up a little better. He wanted her to take better care of her body, "she could put on a little makeup and fix her hair." He seemed to be very stylish and it was obvious that she was older than him. By downplaying her femininity, she looked more like his mother. The Pastor was distraught that he had actually admitted this, but wanted to know how to minister to his wife concerning this.

The church must be careful not to strip women of their God-given *power*. Bubble baths, manicures, pedicures, perfume, roses, gifts and pampering makes us want to be women. This kind of treatment keeps our femininity growing. If this is taken away, we will find something else to replace it.

Most business women or women in leadership or authority roles are very stylish in their dress. They will speak of exercise, spas, fashion and other feminine topics. All of this helps to keep their lion and lamb balanced. When you have to be a lion at work all day, there is nothing better to tame you than a string of pearls or a bouquet of flowers when you get home.

The Curse of the Strong Woman   *Karen Clark-Green*

PART 4

THE CURSE

> Behold, the former things have come to pass, and new things I now declare; before they spring forth I tell you of them.
> Sing to the Lord a new song, and His praise from the end of the earth!
>
> Isaiah 42:9,10 AMP

What is the curse? What is it that plagues strong women and cripples them? The main culprit is that they think they have to be strong, yet they don't know where their strength lies.

Often, as women, we bare more than we have to, do more than we have to and try to be everything to everyone. We hide our pain in order to endure more pain. We see strength as a masculine quality, so we attempt to do what men do. We go into our closets and pull out our tennis shoes, sweats and exercise clothes. All that is missing is our superwoman cape! We can't leap off tall buildings, so why are we trying to?

When I am ministering or performing, a hotel room or suite is usually provided for me. This gives me the privacy that I need to let my real self cry out before God, relax and work the stress out of my life. This, in turn, allows me to hear God more clearly.

Starting in October, 1994, every couple of months a friend would call and say, "You've been on my mind, and the Lord said that you need to get away, so I am providing a room for you when you come to town." Each time it gave me an opportunity to vent my rage.

While attending a conference in Tulsa, Oklahoma, I was thrilled to have a suite to myself so that I could be alone with God. The first night I didn't sleep very well because of the quiet rage within me. The next day, however, I was settled in and immediately God's presence overwhelmed my restless soul. Questions came pouring out, emerging in the form of groans and moans because the pain was too much to verbalize. "Oh, God, why?" I demanded. "Where is the peace, happiness and joy of my salvation? Why is my life so hard and painful? What did I do to deserve this?

It seemed as if the more I cried out to the Lord, the more I needed to cry out. My strong exterior covered me well, but my internal war was about to bring me face to face with myself.

I ministered in worship the first night, finding my peace again. I had a conversation with the Pastor of the church where the conference was held, that changed my spiritual insight. He explained to me that he could see I was only happy and at peace when I was ministering. (I thought that was my secret!) He explained that I had built a protective wall around myself. "You had to do this to keep your sanity," he said. "God is going to peel this off of you."

The curse had me in a cocoon and God was using my capture to bring me into the fullness of life. Everyone witnessed my strength and power in ministry, but I knew the weakness and powerlessness within me.

God met me that weekend. We talked and wrestled for three days and three nights. The Shekinah glory of God kept the room lit each night. If I feel asleep, I would immediately awaken emerged in his holy presence. I realized that I had been tricked, hoodwinked, if you will, beguiled by the enemy and that I had to get my power back to stop the curse.

I had followed all the steps leading up to this point. I was ridiculed, upset, betrayed, abused, laughed at, falsely accused, crucified, dead, spent a good amount of time in hell and now it was time to take the keys and let myself out of bondage. It was time to reign in heavenly places with my Lord.

The song, "Zion Is Calling You To A Higher Place of Praise" rang out like church bells. My soul answered the call and my false, protective life shattered, allowing the real me to step toward the call. I realized that the deep yearning for that higher call started all of the events and upheaval in my life. If I had not answered the call, I would not be feeling like I was. I would have still been in my false, protective, shallow world, not achieving great things for God.

Immediately, another call came from God in song, and yes, I answered! "I will do a new thing in you. Whatever you ask for, whatever you pray for, nothing shall be denied, saith the Lord."

Element Four: *Answer the call to the high place!*

The Curse of the Strong Woman Karen Clark-Green

12

THE WALKING DEAD

Judy, a prophet of God, had just finished ministering to a group of women. God moved mightily She expounded on how God is aligning the Church for the next great move and the important role women will play. I listened very carefully as she mentioned over and over, "Let the past go. Don't look back."

It has always amazed me that many women in the forefront of ministry, on the front lines, or women in the public eye, seem to have in-depth personal problems. Women who have conquered these problems declare and use them in their endeavors. Other women seem to have tucked them away somewhere, so no one can find them. They haven't been destroyed so they still exist. But where are they?

It was clear to me that there were some problems in Judy's marriage, as a mother, and in relationships. Whenever we talked, it was always spiritual. Parts of her life were *off limits*.

While ministering to her after this women's meeting, wounds began to appear that I had never seen before. I prophesied to her of what God was going to do for her once she got these areas together. She stood up, looked at me, straightened her clothes, her hair and her face. Without uttering a word, she just walked off.

"Oh, God, what did I say wrong? What did I do?" I thought I had misinterpreted something or wasn't hearing God clearly. I did not want to hurt my friend. I wanted to help her. As I prayed, God revealed to me that an internal war was going on within Judy. The call on her life necessitated that she move up a level. This yearning for more knowledge of God, success and a better understanding of who she is, had incited a war within her.

An issue or a person who is hurting you or causing you stress and anguish will always remain a flesh wound until you deal with the problem and attempt to resolve it. Judy made a choice to die in the areas that were still painful to her, because she could not afford to feel hurt, stress, or anguish. The internal war will hide, block and deaden until the person can't find the hurt.

I spent years trying to recall parts of my childhood that seemed to have vanished. It was not until I yearned for a close relationship with the Lord that He began to reveal "suicide" to me. There were parts of me that were dead. I was willing to die to avoid feeling the pain.

As I ministered, I listened to others say, "I can't remember that," or "I can't recall most of my childhood. I wonder what that means?" We see the situation as hopeless, because it doesn't make sense to us.

As you can see, our "suicide" has complications. First, we become liars. We say, "I don't hurt." The lie will evolve to, "I will never hurt like this again." Then this statement evolves to, "I will not lose control ever again so I am susceptible to being hurt." We put a divider between the truth and the lie. The divider separates the mind from the agony in the heart, which causes forgetfulness. We are walking, talking, teaching, writing, lecturing, preaching, performing and leading, yet we are dead.

Dead people cannot feel pain, so how do they know pain is occurring? Dead people do not acknowledge what caused their pain, so how do they avoid the cause?

Pain lets you know that you are alive. Have you ever sat on your legs too long or fell asleep on your arm? Numbness occurs because the blood flow has been affected. It is an uncomfortable tingling, dull kind of pain that lets you know something is wrong. If the pain does not occur, you lose all sense of feeling, which will then lead to more serious problems.

We need all of our thought and rationalizing capacities to make sound decisions and to discern wisely. If you were hurt in a relationship the truth will tell you, "I should not allow myself to be vulnerable to being hurt again. My heart craves love to bring me back to life, but is love real? If I show how I really feel to this person, they might reject me, use me, or abuse me. That's what the other person did."

The lie says, "don't trust them, choose the one who is uncommitted, he won't hurt you. Just go for the one night stand because then you can stay in control. Don't open your heart to anyone, or they might arouse passion in you."

You must understand, change will upset your comfort. Facing truths that have always been denied will disrupt your life. Judy didn't understand that her judgments had been distorted. She opened herself up to relationships, family members and coworkers who hurt and victimized her continually. She doesn't know what hurt her, so she is doomed to relive the hurt. She didn't have the ability to judge the present and plan for the future.

A relationship of trust and caring will be frightening to a woman like this because of the risk. Relationships that are not healthy will predominate her life, being hurt again. She will endure the mistreatment and quietly detach herself from those who are misusing and abusing her. These people will think that she is just a quiet person but she is actually avoiding those who cause her pain.

You made the decision to die, now you have to make the decision to live! When you plan for the future, that's life and life promotes healing. Increasing knowledge is life, yearning for a deeper relationship with God is life. Life forces you to deal with the death in you, for you cannot be dead and alive at the same time.

God is in your future, not in your past. The past is nonexistent and only holds death. Choose life!

13

THE BROKEN HEART

> Search me, O God, and know my heart: try me, and know my thoughts:
> And see if there be any wicked way in me, and lead me in the way everlasting.
> **Psalm 139:23,24**

> A merry heart maketh a cheerful countenance: but by sorrow of the heart the spirit is broken.
> **Proverbs 15:13**

> A merry heart doeth good like a medicine: but a broken spirit drieth the bones.
> **Proverbs 17:22**

A broken heart will drive you to something your body can't handle. A broken heart is the most treacherous enemy a strong woman can have. A woman with a broken heart is not free to reach her full potential. A broken heart drives you to commit emotional suicide or exist in pain. She will be stuck in self-defeating behavior, not having the proper insight into what makes her behave a certain way. Perhaps if we disclose some of the causes of this enemy, it will help us realize our need for healing.

Most of our negatives were developed by the age of five. All of the important information about the world and life was received from our families. Our emotional foundation was built in the safety of our home or with our immediate loved ones. A child learns by how you treat them, how they see you treat others and how you resolve problems.

Proverbs 22:6 says, *Train up a child in the way he should go: and when he is old, he will not depart from it.* If a child is trained in the way that he shouldn't go, will he also not depart from it when he is old? The wrong training is not intentional, but children learn the wrong things by the example of their parents and other immediate family members. If a parent never says, I'm sorry, the child learns to do the same thing. If the parent is argumentative, the child will be the same way. The child can be disciplined and taught correct behavior. The adult will make excuses or justify his actions.

Webster defines *dysfunctional* as "impaired or abnormal behavior." When you are in the midst of the functioning of a family, it will appear normal because this is the life that you are experiencing on a day to day basis. Love and a sense of security are learned or not learned in the home. Holding a baby makes him or her feel secure. We have all heard our grandmothers and mothers say, " Stop holding that baby, or let that baby cry so you won't spoil them."

Babies become emotionally strong by your touch. Hold them as often as you can. Make them feel secure in love, or when they are older, they go searching for it. Lap time, which is sufficient time on your mother's or father's lap, is vital. Otherwise, sex, drugs, food, and other venues will plague their adult lives.

The parental relationship is so important to a child. And since we are speaking of females, the father-daughter relationship is the most crucial relationship to her womanhood. It is important for adults to understand that when we remember or reminisce about our childhood, we remember what the child remembers. It will be from the child's point of view, so it may not be accurate. A child in a bad, unpleasant, or troubled home setting can protect himself by promising that he will do a better job when he grows up.

A young woman learns about relationships from her parents - how to act, how to communicate and how to choose. Don't you find it interesting when a young girl says, "I want to marry someone just like my daddy" or, "I don't want a man like my father." No matter what the declaration, usually they end up with someone "just like daddy," even when they put forth great effort not to. Her father represents "male" to her - how to be treated, how to be taken care of, how to be talked to and how not to be talked to.

I have spoken with many women who didn't realize they had a man like daddy. Even when they experienced the first butterflies in their stomach - the same feeling of fear they had whenever they were in trouble with their fathers - they didn't realize where that feeling came from.

How a father shows love and respect to a female child will, to a large extent, determine her self-worth. How a father treats the female child's mother will determine her self-respect.

Mary Ellen

Mary Ellen could not remember being held by her father. She remembers severe discipline, strictness and how he yelled at her mother. She recalled bouts of his jealousy towards her mother and the arguments when he accused her of getting attention from other men.

Mary Ellen learned from her father that attention from men was a bad thing. She added, "He never held my mother or me or told us that he loved us." Just because she couldn't remember does not mean that it didn't happen. It just did not balance out or outweigh the negatives that her father gave.

In her personality, she developed a knowledge that men are demanding, hurtful and when they pay too much attention to you, you are doing something wrong. Mary Ellen was always in wrong, destructive relationships with men, still searching for that father-daughter bond.

Since father is the strength and security in the home, it is important to have his love. Her father was a good provider and often brought gifts. This act told Mary Ellen that he loved her. When she was bad, she did not get a gift. It was in these times that she didn't feel loved. Her relationships included a fear of not being loved, or doing something wrong to make him not love her.

Tina

Tina's mother never got married, yet many men were interested in her. Her mother, a professional woman, only dated professional men. Tina's relationships with her grandfather and uncles were good. They always made her feel special. She paid close attention to the kind of men that her mom dated, searching for that missing element in her life.

Tina saw her father but never spent a lot of time with him. Internally, she was angry with him for not being there and for not being what her mother wanted him to be. Tina's expectations from men were high. She got engaged before she graduated from high school, and planned to marry the following year. She was not ready for marriage. She had no idea who she was, but she was determined not to live alone like her mother. Tina was determined not to let her man get away with the things that her mother allowed to be done to her.

The way mother relates or handles father is an expression of what it means to be a woman. Positive and negative explanations of womanhood are constantly put into the daughter's mind. A mother who overworks, doing her job and the father's, is teaching the daughter to do the same thing.

A father comes home from a distressing day at work. His temper is short, and it doesn't take much for him to explode. The mother forgets to give him an important message, and he angrily flies into a rage, swearing, screaming and attacking her self-worth. How the mother handles this is crucial to the daughter's development as a woman. If she swears and fights back, she is giving the message that this is the answer to this kind of behavior. On the other hand, submitting to this kind of behavior gives the message of submitting to rage and anger from men. A wise woman will realize the life-altering effects her decisions make on her daughter.

A child's mind cannot handle the fact that a parent cannot protect or provide for them. If mother cannot protect herself, *how can she protect me,* will be the cry of the child. This will cause a child to go into a "I must protect myself" mode, and the child will become quiet and distant, trying to hide from pain.

When abuse of any kind is added to this picture, in-depth degrees of secrecy and shame are also added.

Jane

Jane was one of those superwomen who people looked at in amazement, wondering, "How does she do it?" Energetically, she pops from one agenda to another, taking care of her husband, children and home, trying to balance these responsibilities with her career. As a working mom, she tries to make parent-teacher conferences and keep everyone happy.

There is no way a good Christian woman would be this busy and not be as busy for the Lord. So she serves in a ministry position in her church, serving on two or more committees, teaches Sunday school, serves soup at shelters and sings in the choir. What a woman! Is she the example we should follow? Let's interview her and see what she says:

Interviewer: How do you manage to give so much of yourself to others?

Jane: I am being the cheerful giver that the Word of God says we are to be.

Interviewer: I don't see how you have time to sleep. Do you get a full night's sleep? Is that your secret?

Jane: Well, no. Sometimes I only get four or five hours of sleep, but I am used to it, or my body has adjusted. As mothers, our bodies never regain all the rest we lost when our children were babies, so we adjust.

Interviewer: It must make you feel very good to be able to do so much for God. He must give you supernatural strength.

Jane: Well, no. In fact, at the end of the day, I am so exhausted from the variety of things that I have to do, I sometimes wonder if I will make it. If I don't do it, though, who will? There are many times that I don't get to some vital task with my job, and I ran around like crazy this week, trying to make a cake for my son's birthday, which I never did get to do. I had to buy one.

Interviewer: The Scripture does say, **...For unto whomsoever much is given, of him shall be much required** (Luke 12:48).

Jane:	That's true, but that same Scripture also says, "And even more will be heaped upon you."
Interviewer:	Do you often find that you become stressed with all of the responsibilities that you have?
Jane:	Yes! I need a vacation, but everyone expects so much from me. If I did get away, I would just have more work waiting on me when I returned.
Interviewer:	Let someone else do it.
Jane:	But it's my job.
Interviewer:	God never intended for one woman to do everything.
Jane:	I am not trying to do everything. I have to do my job and take care of my responsibilities.
Interviewer:	What would happen if you didn't do your job, if one day you decided, "I'm just going to rest today, take care of myself and get some ministry to relieve my stress?"
Jane:	I would feel very guilty.
Interviewer:	What happens when you do get behind? How do you handle it? Can you be very honest with me?

Jane:	Usually, I cry and ask God, "Is this it? Is this what my life is all about? Is this the joy of my salvation?"
Interviewer:	Do you have a fight with depression, since you have all of this pressure on you?
Jane:	Yes, but no one sees it, except my husband and children. Usually, I end up yelling at them to make it not so apparent.
Interviewer:	I would like to pray for strength and wisdom for you. God would never put more on you than you can bear. You can't make others' lives better by killing yourself. Christ already died for them. You don't have to. Can you describe some of the true feelings that you have in your heart right now?
Jane:	Loneliness, hopelessness, grief, anger, despair, guilt, fear, hate and rage! I'm trying so hard, why does it hurt so bad?
Interviewer:	Your heart is broken. You cannot physically be all things to all people. If you do everyone's job, you cripple them and make them handicapped. At some point, you will mature enough to say "no" and not care what anyone else thinks about it! You are not a **superwoman**, and you don't have to be perfect.

Jane: I feel better now that I got that out. I was mad at God, because I felt that He put all of this on me. I was mad at myself for not being able to do it.

Interviewer: Confession and forgiveness are essential for healing a broken heart. You can stop trying to hide your broken heart under more work. Take some personal time, find out who you really are, not who you became - *and start living!*

Jane: Thank you. Now I am ready to pray.

Proverbs 25:20 says, **"As he that taketh away a garment in cold weather, and as vinegar upon nitre, so is he that singeth songs to an heavy heart."** The only way your life will change is for your broken heart to be healed. I've spoken to many women who appear to have it all together, myself included, women who are secretly brokenhearted. This is the curse at work.

Writing this book was a difficult task because of the emotional impact. Not only have I lived the issues of the book, but as I spoke with women, did research and conversed with medical experts, I had to relive the pain again myself. As I began to write, all of the emotions resurfaced so that compassion could come through my writing. This section on the curse was most difficult. I had to examine every emotional pain that was coming forth in order to expose it.

For the three weeks that I spent just trying to write all of the information down like I wanted it to appear, I became depressed, stressed and angry. I ate everything I could put my hands on. I began to wear more makeup at certain times and at other times I didn't care what I looked like. Being an actress, I have been trained to become the person in the role, so I became all of these people and felt what they feel. Now that I am done with this, I can go wash my face, go on a diet and move on to the next section.

Why did I react this way? I have been doing it all of my life, but I just didn't understand why. I learned that my broken heart, triggered by emotions, made me eat more in an attempt to bury my anger, depression, sadness, frustration and other strong feelings under food. I went back to the child, who in my mother's care was fed, warmed and comforted in a secure, loving place. This is the same feeling we get when we agonize over something, and we feel the need to lay down or rest. We curl up in a fetal position, often holding our stomach, taking us back to the safety of the womb, loved in our mother's care.

The additional makeup helped me to hide my dissatisfaction with myself and with life and fulfilled the need to feel more like a woman. I needed to feel loved, pampered and cherished. As women, we know that makeup is a healthy part of who we are, but we can also make it unhealthy if we are not careful.

Women with broken hearts are usually out of control. They experience depression and major bouts with stress. They are women who are overweight, bulimic, anorexic, women who have drug problems, relationship problems, promiscuity problems, or sex problems. They are women who can't seem to fit, have low self-esteem and low self worth. They are women who are people-pleasers and who overwork to hide their lack as women. These women rarely make correct choices.

Psalm 119:80 says, "**Let my heart be sound in thy statutes; that I be not ashamed.**" Their way of thinking must be changed after their heart is healed. It has to be cognitively restructured. Their thinking must be changed, or should I say, they need a paradigm shift so their response to a particular situation is different. Abuse, rejection and self-protection break the heart, while confession and forgiveness heal it.

Our hearts have been damaged, wounded, or torn, and only spiritual surgery can bring healing and wholeness.

When the doctors go in to remove a cancer, the pain is so severe that you need an anesthetic to numb the pain. The problem is removed, then the healing process begins. Anyone who has had surgery knows that healing hurts. As the pain begins to subside, you realize that you are getting better.

When your heart has been broken, your ability to trust has been affected. Through confession and forgiveness towards God, yourself and others, the hardening of your heart will begin to break up and be softened. This will also help your family to heal, because the pain of a brokenhearted woman will show up in her family.

You cannot move on until you deal with your broken heart.

14

Eanie, Meanie, Minee, Mo, Will My Mate Be Friend or Foe?

> And hath made of one blood all nations of men for to dwell on all the face of the earth, and hath determined the times before appointed, and the bounds of their habitation.
>
> **Acts 17:26**

I hear many people speak of finding their soul mate, someone they are compatible with who loves the same things and has similar goals and interests. When looking for Mr. Right, you need to know what to look for.

Our spirit is made for close communication and friendship with God. Nothing and no one else can fill that void, for we were created to seek God. Our primary purpose is to seek Him and fellowship with Him. You can hook up with someone, and the effects of that relationship will go on years after the relationship ends. If you are not married, do not become involved in any relationship to the point of emotional involvement unless you plan to spend the rest of your life with that person. It will affect your life, your children's lives and your children's children's lives.

Sex makes spiritual covenants. As women, we do not look at sex in the correct context. We bond through sex. When a woman gives into a man and has a sexual relationship without commitment, there is nothing to commit to. Her act of having sex is the totality of giving *all* of herself to a man. The only way she does not give all of herself is if she has moved into the lion mode, which means she is stuck and the lamb qualities are lost. In the spirit, she has formed a covenant. So, even though love may not exist, when she separates from this individual, the results are as painful as a divorce, because the two that became one are now being torn apart.

Premarital sex weakens the marriage bond, and you take the weakness into your marriage. Two people attracted to each other who decide, "maybe this is someone I would like to spend my life with," must first learn how to be friends.

A young dating couple I know is having a hard time not, "going all the way." They have been together for two months and feel that they deserve to be rewarded. No commitment has been made, nonetheless, they are having a battle with their flesh. Their relationship is shallow.

Another older male and female, who are attracted to each other, are learning how to be friends. They have developed an in-depth respect, appreciation and carefulness with each other. They are challenged by their sexual attraction to each other, but they have learned the power of intimacy that puts a relationship on another level.

To be intimate emotionally and intellectually builds a commitment level that takes part of one and gives it to the other; from the man to the woman and from the woman to the man. The deeper you share with each other, the more emotionally involved you become. This helps you determine where you fit in this person's life. It is not determined by good or bad sex!

Today, many couples have problems in their marriage because thirty five years ago, while in high school, they had sex. She buried her resentment within herself, but two years into the marriage, the resentment surfaced and they have been having problems ever since.

It is impossible to bestow something on someone else if you have not felt the fruit of it. We must learn to be intimate to one's self.

Marriage is not an arrangement of persons, but *a divine act of God.* It is a mystery, a sacrament, an unexplainable act. How can two people become one flesh? To compliment and complete each other, marriage must be a divine act.

A family unit is the most expeditious way to extend the Kingdom of God. Our choices are vital to the completion of God's plan. It is to be hoped that with this understanding we will be more careful with choices in relationships.

I have put together a section on couples and the effects that the qualities *strong and weak* have on men and women in relationships. For too long, we have been ignorant in what to look for in finding a mate.

Divorce and living together are prevalent marriage alternatives these days. I believe this is a cry for better relationships and deeper commitments. Dissatisfaction occurs because marital expectations are greater than they were in the past. This section will help you look for the right qualities in yourself, your mate, or in your prospective mate.

We have taken this saying, "falling in love," as the method to be in love. Love is not something you fall into. *Falling* denotes being out of control, something you cannot help doing. If one or both parties involved *are falling,* one or both are guaranteed to get hurt.

You go into love with both eyes open and with a clear mind. You make the decision to *walk into love,* not fall. Let it be your choice. Once you have committed your love to each other and taken the relationship to the next level, your way of relating to each other should go to the next level, too.

Women, remember, once you are conquered, do not expect your mate to keep courting you. Usually, men move on to the next level of relating, while women still want to be courted.

With couples who have been together for years without marriage, the men are in the marital style of relating, while the women are still in the courtship style of relating. The man's method of keeping the woman is different than his method of getting her.

Weak Man/Weak Woman

It is very difficult for a relationship to work without working on it. When you are coupled with someone who has the same weaknesses you do, there is almost no chance for growth.

A weak man and a weak woman together will only achieve to a certain point. They will make excuses for each other's weaknesses and will not be achievers. They will probably be the nice couple who never bother anyone. They will be dependable and always give for rummage sales, always making donations for whatever the cause may be. They will always ask you to pray for them. They may be judgmental, gossipers, complainers, two busybodies who agree with the faults of others. You will always see them together.

The damaging part is, they do not help each other grow. They do not bother the devil, and he in turn does not bother them. Unfortunately, because of this, they are often used by the devil.

The weak woman will try to control her man. She is the woman who became a mother and forgot how to be a woman. She does everything for her man, working hard to look as if she has it all together. The more she does, the more she complains. She literally becomes the nurturer. His weak man tendencies probably stem from childhood, where he did not have the responsibility of suffering consequences for his actions, but was often rescued by his mother. The mother may have put the son's well-being ahead of her own husband, until she raises a son who does not grow into healthy manhood.

The weak man expects the woman to take care of him, to make his dinner, make the bed, pay the bills, plan the vacation, plan social events, pick him up, pick up his socks and solve problems. He will not be able to protect, give back, develop, or cherish. He will complain of always making up first, and will match the woman's every complaint. His masculine power has now become a feminine weakness.

Strong Man/Weak Woman

A strong man knows who he is. A strong man has dreams and visions that he will work overtime to fulfill. He will take care of his woman, because he understands what she is for. He will force her to move. He will cherish her, and he will dress and provide for her. It makes him look good, it's supposed to. He is the man you see opening doors for her, buying gifts for her and supporting her dreams.

The weak woman will complain, challenge him and act as if she cannot do anything, especially if it is something that she does not want to do. If she wants to do it, she will continue without him and become selfish. A weak woman will challenge his visions and dreams. She will accuse him of not including her, and she will zap his strength. They will look good in public and be successful because of him. Behind closed doors, she will be a sore to him!

The strong man wants to give, protect and cherish. He enjoys developing projects, people and anything else that affects his life. A weak woman will take this as criticism and will not receive with joy. Instead, she will argue word for word to discount his perception. The weak woman may want equality until she destroys her femininity and sexual attractiveness. The weak woman may be successful at her business and may even make as much money, if not more, than her strong man. This will cause the weak woman to fight to be respected instead of understanding that the strong man wants to cherish her. All the strong man really wants is for his woman to trust him.

The weak woman will appear strong and aggressive to others, mistaking this quality for strength. It is a fear of not being able to be in control, so like any spoiled brat, her temper tantrums will vary and continue until she gets her way.

Strong Woman/Weak Man

Unfortunately, in our society today, this is the common grouping - strong woman/weak man - that couples fit into.

A strong woman with a weak man will make the man dependent on her for strength. This will eventually break the will of the strong woman. They will appear strong because of her strength.

Proverbs 31:23 says, **Her husband is known in the gates, when he sitteth among the elders of the land.** When the woman finally realizes that she has sacrificed her life to build his, it will probably be too late to salvage his potential. Upon the realization of the woman, she will either continue to take up his slack, which will be the ultimate sacrifice, or not continue to take up the slack, which will expose him.

By taking up his slack, she has now stunted his future growth and made him more dependent on her. Most women will continue this out of pride rather than out of love. They feel trapped and angry at God and unable to forgive themselves, so they merely exist. Their strength and pride, which become collaborators, will put on a coping mechanism that will help them to be successful at this endeavor.

On the other hand, the strong woman who makes the decision not to take up his slack, will cause him to be exposed. This could be something as simple as giving him the responsibility of picking up his clothes off the floor, or as complicated as making sure his business does not fail because of his neglect and mistakes. It will be mandatory for his existence to mature and begin to develop on his own, or his life will end. This will happen because he has never been able to exist on his own. The longer the man is in this state, the more at risk he is for survival.

The strong woman has used her enabling behavior to allow the man to get away with something that he deserves to suffer the consequences for. For example, a husband who refuses to go to work deserves to lose his job; an alcoholic who drives drunk deserves to get arrested for drunk driving. This does not mean that they are bad people. It simply means that consequences are the only thing that will help them to change.

The strong woman who always rescues the weak man will keep herself off course. She will hurt and feel guilty for not fulfilling her duties. If she is married, she will feel as if she is the one who has failed the marriage. The truth is, you are in a frightening situation that is either threatening your life or future and the enabling behavior helps you feel as if you are in control for a period of time.

The sad part is, the more you rescue the weak man, the more he will need it. He will then begin to feel guilty and resentful towards your efforts. The ultimate danger for the strong woman is becoming cold and uncaring towards the weak man. When this happens, usually it means that you have given up your power or inner strength.

Strong Man/Strong Woman

The strong man and the strong woman are the ideal couple. All of us are strong men and women in our real state. That is why God wants us whole.

A strong man and a strong woman can take over the world. Hitler had a strong woman around him, and he thought he could take over the world. Patrick Kennedy had Rose Kennedy, and Bill Clinton has Hillary. President Clinton knows what he has. That is why he is President. (He is known in the gates of the land because of her.)

The stronger the man, the more gentle he is. He does not have to prove his strength. Weak men are abusive, jealous, argumentative and insecure. John, the disciple, was a strong man. He was the only man out of the disciples to be at the crucifixion with the women. He was tenderhearted. He understood love, which can only come from strength. (John is the one who taught on love.)

The strong man and the strong woman keep each other moving and achieving. The strong man is the one you see cherishing his wife, exalting her, not covering up her mistakes. When the man is strong, the woman will not be bound with taking up his slack. He will protect her femininity, because he understands the purpose and conditions for which she was created. She is the woman who can call her man "lord," because he loves her as his own body.

The strong man will help his woman. He is not afraid of housework. He knows how to cook, and he will take up her slack. He knows his responsibilities as a man and will be adamant about fulfilling them. This will cause the strong woman to love and want to pamper him.

A weak man cannot handle too much pampering. He will stop doing his job just to be pampered. He does not realize that doing his job is what causes the woman to want to pamper him in the first place. A strong woman builds a reputation for her man, whether he is weak or strong. She'll sit at his feet, bathe him, soothe him and do anything else she can for him. He knows her strength is for him, and she does not have to worry about her security, for without security you are not free to be a woman.

The strong man and the strong woman will make sure each other reaches their goals, and will award each other for reaching them. They know when the other is happy or sad, even when they are not together. This is because of the in-depth honesty that they have with each other that only strong people can handle.

A strong man and a strong woman will be a wise man and a wise woman. A strong woman, who is usually a career woman, will not sacrifice her womanhood for her career. She will make herself available for her man, in work, home, play and quiet time. The strong man and woman together will be the perfect balance of his giving and her receiving. It will be a pleasure for him to give to his woman, and the strong woman will take joy in surrendering. A strong man will keep his commitments to the best of his ability, because he wants to be respected. He is focused and knows exactly what he wants.

The strong woman is secure in her womanhood and has learned to love herself. She knows what, when and how much to give. The strong man and woman may be strict in their beliefs, but sensitive in expressing them. Even when the other does not agree, they fight fair.

The strong man and woman understand that to stay strong, they must constantly change, grow and evolve. There is always more to live and more to learn.

The Curse of the Strong Woman   *Karen Clark-Green*

15
WHAT GOD EXPECTS FROM GODLY WOMEN

We must learn survival skills, but we must first become healthy - spiritually, mentally and emotionally.

We must set limits for ourselves and not be afraid to say "no." We must stop allowing guilt to make us think we are the answer to everyone's problems.

When you are married to a man you are enabling or mothering, it makes you feel that you must take care of him. There will be areas where you begin to do the man's responsibilities because he won't. The more you do his duties, the more masculine you will become. Now functioning as a man, you will eventually become the man you wished you had, forgetting how to be a woman.

Here are a few strategies that you can pursue to become the godly woman God has ordained you to be:

1. Examine your good qualities.

Strong women tend to get into self-bashing, a method that says, "What's the use?" It's a method of giving up before you begin. We become martyrs and put our lives, goals, wants and desires on a back burner. This makes us lose faith in our own qualities that would enable us to fulfill our dreams and visions.

Write down your gifts, talents and good points. Then reactivate your faith in yourself. Once you do this and can visually see your value, then you can begin to work on using these qualities again.

2. Learn to relax at home.

Find a place in your house or apartment, even if it is the time you spend in the bathtub, and just relax.

Today's woman has to give on her job, which is a masculine quality. When she comes home, instead of moving back into her feminine role of receiving, she continues to give and becomes burned out. This can also happen when you work in the home if your mindset is that of giving instead of receiving.

Learn to rest! Tired women usually use their time to worry and figure out how they did not accomplish everything of the day. This will disrupt rest and make you feel as if you must force yourself to do more.

At the end of the work day, a man will feel as if he has done his part and is now ready to sit and relax, doing less. As women, our power lies in being receivers, while the man's is in giving. We must decide to make our quiet time a relaxed time so we can move back into our feminine role.

Women, as well as men, want to be loved and appreciated at the end of a long day

3. Know what you stand for.

You may think you don't let other people take advantage of you. However, if you find yourself in situations where you are slowly being pulled into accepting hurtful and unfair behavior, you may unknowingly be showing other people that you are willing to be manipulated.

Women need to set personal boundaries and refuse to compromise. This will help to stop the enabling and mothering. Make a vow to yourself that you will stop covering up other family members' problems, mistakes and addictions. Never do anything that jeopardizes taking care of your health. Make up your mind not to allow abuse of any kind to you or your children. Be firm in your acclamation. Stay away from gossip for it robs integrity, power and inner beauty.

4. Learn to love yourself first.

We must take care of ourselves. Stress, anger and unforgiveness can physically wear the body out. That is why it is so important for you to talk to people. Don't keep these types of feelings inside. Don't bury or hide them, because it will make your body sick.

Medical and psychiatric reports describe a list of illnesses that result from an inability to deal with emotional distress - backaches, muscle spasms, general body tightness, tension headaches, migraine headaches, ulcers, colitis, chronic indigestion, various types of bowel disorders, high blood pressure and coronary diseases.

I will briefly touch on depression, because we need to understand, particularly as women, how deadly depression can be.

Often, we say, "Oh, I'm depressed," not realizing that this statement is serious. How do we know when it is a case of chronic depression? Carefully examine yourself from the following list of symptoms:

* Constantly feeling tired

* Lack of enthusiasm

* Inability to feel pleasure or joy

* Sleeping long hours

* Crying for no reason

* Suicidal fantasies

* Insomnia

* Spending too much time thinking in the past hopelessness

* Extreme irritability

* Neglect of appearance

Many women have preexisting tendencies towards depression because of their childhood. Soil that is fertile for chronic depression to bloom is characterized by pain, confusion, loss of confidence, repressed rage and powerlessness.

The Curse of the Strong Woman   *Karen Clark-Green*

PART 5

FREE AT LAST

> And ye shall know the truth, and the truth shall make you free.
> **John 8:32**

I didn't know exactly how I should end the book. Whenever we tell a story, we look for endings, preferably a happy ending. The journey that I was on in life was definitely taking me somewhere, I just wasn't sure where that place was.

My emotions were so involved in all of the things that had happened to me and all of the women that I had spoken to. How would our healing or deliverance or freedom to be the real person God intended us to be manifest?

The Lord made one fact very clear to me, that is, deliverance is *never* in the soulish area, because we are spirit. Your spirit is already made free, you just need to come out of your emotions to realize this. As I emerged, my true nature took over. As spirit, I'm already made free.

It is very important to constantly communicate with God in order to get the directions needed to complete the task. I had just found my last element of what God expects from godly women.

Element Five: *Stay connected to God.*

16

SPIRIT, SOUL AND BODY

We are made up of three parts - spirit, soul and body. Let's look briefly at each of these areas.

Spirit

The Holy Spirit relates us to God and makes us conscious of Him. And because God wants us to be like Him, He created us in His likeness and image.

> And God said, Let us make man in our image, after our likeness: and let them have dominion over the fish of the sea, and over the fowl of the air, and over the cattle, and over all the earth, and over every creeping thing that creepeth upon the earth.
> So God created man in his own image, in the image of God created he him; male and female created he them
> And the Lord God formed man of the dust of the ground, and breathed into his nostrils the breath of life; and man became a living soul.
> Genesis 1:26,27; 2:7

To make is the Hebrew word *asha,* which means "to form something out of something that already exists." Genesis 1:27 says, **"So God created man in his own image,...."** The word *create* in Hebrew is *brera,* which means "to form out of nothing."

The term, *formed man,* expresses the relationship of a craftsman to his material. The verb *formed* is used on occasion for the potter (Jeremiah 18:2) and man represents the clay, connoting skill. The *potter* sets the design and pattern. The corporeal part was *the dust of the ground,* and the non corporeal part was *the breath of life.* The word *breath* in Hebrew is *ruach,* which means "spirit."

Therefore, man is spirit, even as God is Spirit. The spirit is your true essence. Or, we could say it this way: *The spirit that God breathed into you is the real you.*

Too many of us are not led by our spirits, but by our flesh. We know the good in us, the difference between right and wrong. But somehow we still struggle to obey God. Even Jesus said to His disciples in the garden of Gethsemane, ...**the spirit indeed is willing, but the flesh is weak** (Matthew 26:41). He said this when the disciples could not stay awake to watch and keep guard when He prayed.

As women, the circumstances of everyday living pull on us, especially as wives and mothers. When we detach ourselves from our spirit, we are then controlled by our mind and emotions. Our emotions, particularly, can get us into all kinds of trouble and also cause us to think irrationally.

The Greek word *psyche* translates "heart." The actual translation is, *the core of the spirit.* Many things can happen to our body, such as illness, amputation, scaring, etc. But these things cannot harm the spirit of a person. Your body may die physically, but your spirit will live forever. Your heart may be broken, but your spirit is still intact.

How do we combat depression, anxiety and the blues? *By staying connected to God* with our spirit. Sometimes I use what I call my "tootsie roll pop plan." The tootsie roll in the middle is the spirit or the real me. The candy around the tootsie roll is just a covering. Any attacks that come must hit the hard candy shell, and if you forget that's not really you, you will crack. The hard candy may chip, split, or even melt, but the tootsie roll is not harmed.

The fulfillment of the plan of God for the Body of Christ is dependent upon knowing who you are as a woman, your importance, purpose and place. In order for the next *move* of God to happen, women must get into position. Remember, *you were uniquely created for a "special" task!*

Soul

The soul, made up of the mind, will and emotions, relates us to ourselves and gives us consciousness.

Hurts and disappointments are very real. When our minds are focused on the Lord, He keeps us in perfect peace, and our emotions will not overwhelm us.

Isaiah 26:3 says, **Thou wilt keep him in perfect peace, whose mind is stayed on thee: because he trusteth in thee.** It is the devil's job to get our minds off of the Lord. Why? Then we will not have peace. Where is peace housed? In the soul or emotions.

Genesis 2:7 says, **And the Lord God formed man of the dust of the ground, and breathed into his nostrils the breath of life; and man became a living soul.**

After the breath of life entered into man's nostrils and the spirit and body were joined, man became a living soul. Our soul includes the emotions, personality and human characteristics. The soul has the power of choosing to make us happy and content (peaceful) or choosing not to be happy and content, allowing depression, stress, or anxiety to affect us negatively.

I am amazed at the power of the mind. If we have a pain that is too much to bear, we bury it and don't even remember the incident. On the other hand, we can apply pain to an incident to justify why we hurt. As a result, we are left without peace.

When your mind is not on the Lord, your mind is occupied with *you* and what you are going through - your problems, likes and dislikes, physical pains, financial pains, spiritual pains, relationship problems, on-the-job problems, marriage problems and any other problems that you can conjure up. As women, we tend to be more emotional than men. But our emotions must always be under the lordship of Jesus Christ and guided by the Holy Spirit, or we will be taken on an emotional roller coaster ride that will literally destroy us.

John 8:31,32 says:
Then said Jesus to those Jews which believed on him, If ye continue in my word, then are ye my disciples indeed;
And ye shall know the truth, and the truth shall make you free.

Most of us have suppressed truth. People who cannot remember parts of their lives are hiding from incidents that are too painful or traumatic to deal with, so they bury them. Only the truth can make you free. If you are not willing to face the truth, you will not get free. We can adjust to being happy or content in a state or situation where we feel there is no way out. This is a method of protecting oneself from pain.

In John 8:31,32, Jesus was speaking to Jews who:
1) Believed on Him; and
2) Then He said, **If ye continue in my word,** which means their minds were occupied with Jesus and the Word of God. This allowed peace to enter because their minds were stayed on the Lord.

As a result: 1) You shall know the truth; and
2) The truth shall make you free.

It seems hard for us to understand why a battered wife would stay with a man who hurts her physically, emotionally, sexually, or verbally. Do these women have peace to even realize the truth of their situations? Or, have they buried the truth because their lives are so painful? In order to stay in such a situation, you must adjust, pretend, or lie to yourself to be able to bear the pain. People do this when they feel there is no way out.

Peace is a prerequisite to knowing the truth and being made free. In order to get peace, your mind must be stayed on the Lord, believing on Him and continuing in His Word. When God cannot obtain your attention through the word, you head for oppression and captivity by the enemy.

As women, usually we are very sensitive to the spiritual world. Therefore, we must find the stairway to peace and freedom, especially because our bodies often go through hormonal swings.

Depression

Webster describes *depression* as, "A state of being depressed; a state of feeling sad; a psycho-neurotic or psychotic disorder marked by sadness, decrease in appetite (sometimes an increase,) time spent sleeping or in bed, feelings of dejection and hopelessness, and sometimes suicidal tendencies; a lowering of vitality or functional level."

Statistics say that one-fourth of all women have at some time in their lives been depressed. Depression occurs in a mind without peace. According to Dr. Ellen McGrath, Ph.D., Chairwoman of the American Psychological Association Task Force on Women and Depression, there are seven million women in the U. S. with diagnosable depression. Why? Because women are thinkers and we think about what we feel. We will try to figure out why we are in the mood we are in and whose fault it is. We become introverted with our thoughts and capture all of our emotional problems in our body, which, in turn, makes us ill. We need to learn to have more activity or play time to release some of the depression. We must also learn not to spend so much time occupying our minds with ourselves.

Studies show that women have double the risk for depression than men. Risk factors for women include physical and sexual abuse, menopause, menstruation and childbirth. Many females experience some form of molestation, rape, or sexual abuse before the age of twenty-one. Experts believe that over 50 percent of the female population have experienced this type of behavior.

The effects of the mental and emotional damage may not manifest until years later, in marriage, or in other relationships.

According to the American Psychological Association, women in unhappy marriages are more likely to suffer chronic depression.

Depression, stress and anxiety are normally treated by medication and counseling. All of us at some time will need help dealing with the ups and downs that life offers. As children of God, we have authority over the enemy, but simple knowledge of the Word of God will make us free.

> **Thou wilt keep him in perfect peace, whose mind is stayed on thee: because he trusteth in thee.**
> **Isaiah 26:3**

> **If ye continue in my word, then are ye my disciples indeed;**
> **And ye shall know the truth, and the truth shall make you free.**
> **John 8:31, 32**

Body

The body relates us to our physical needs. First Corinthians 3:16,17 says:

Know ye not that ye are the temple of God, and that the Spirit of God dwelleth in you?

If any man defile the temple of God, him shall God destroy; for the temple of God is holy, which temple ye are.

We are spirit, soul and body, and most Christians feel that God is not concerned about the body. This, of course, is not true, for the Lord had a great desire for a house so He could dwell among men.

In Exodus 25:8 God said to Moses, **And let them make me a sanctuary; that I may dwell among them.** The tabernacle was constructed in three parts: the Holy of Holies, the sanctuary and the outer court. The human tabernacle is also constructed in three parts: spirit, soul and body.

When we talk about dying to the flesh, we are not talking about the body but about our attitude toward sin. The flesh and the physical body are two different things.

Our physical body does not lead us into sin, but lust, an un-renewed mind and wrong attitudes do.

What does God expect from us concerning the *body?*

Most Christians, especially those in the United States, eat according to taste and desire and do not understand the necessity of life that food contains. Food is the fuel we need to keep our bodies strong, so that we may be able to do the work of God's Kingdom.

We plan our meals according to budget or desire instead of according to what is good for us. Jesus gave dietary instructions to the seventy disciples that He sent forth. He said, **"And in the same house remain, eating and drinking such things as they give... eat such things as are set before you."** (Luke 10:7,8)

Women are very sensitive about their appearance, especially about their weight. We will change our diet for appearance, which is vanity, but rarely for spiritual reasons.

Proverbs 31:30 AMP says, **"Charm and grace are deceptive, and beauty is vain [because it is not lasting], but a woman who reverently and worshipfully fears the Lord, she shall be praised!"**

During the summer of 1988, 1 spent some time in Milano, Italy, studying with my vocal coach. Our diet was mainly vegetables, since Italians are not big meat eaters. Many of the simple and unfamiliar vegetarian meals were very hard for me to eat. Daily, at each meal, I could hear the Lord clearly say, "Eat such things as are set before you." So I did.

I can remember wanting meat so badly. I was constantly busy, three months pregnant and fighting a spiritual battle that I did not know existed. By the fourth day I smelled meat cooking and I got excited. When it was time for dinner to be served, I was ready. I am not a seafood eater, because I do not have a tolerance for the oil taste of seafood. What most people do not know is, Italians are big seafood eaters. They eat all kinds of seafood.

The gumbo of seafood was to be eaten over pasta. When I could not identify some of the strange creatures in the pot, I became fearful. I intently waited to hear the Lord's words, "Eat such things as are set before you."

As I waited with tears in my eyes, my host looked at me and said, "You really don't care for seafood, do you?" What a relief! But it was another day without meat. The spiritual battle that I had encountered had heightened by this time. If I had eaten like I was used to eating, I would not have had the strength to endure the physical or spiritual strain.

Most of us spend our whole lives on a continuous diet, with little progress. The reasons are all wrong. While we are dieting and watching what we eat, we continue to feed our families the wrong thing. Our husband's physical health begins to drop, his energy begins to fade, his tolerance and general attitude begin to change as his body changes. Our children become unruly, complain about headaches, tiredness and body pains. Somehow, we still don't realize that these bodies house the Holy Spirit, and we must take care of them.

Our appearance should not determine how and when we serve the Lord. Too much weight can make you feel like not standing in front of people. It will definitely tell you that you don't have anything to wear!

We do not like to call things as they really are. Americans have a problem with gluttony. Proverbs 23:21 says, **"For the drunkard and the glutton shall come to poverty."** *Notice, drunkard and glutton* are usually used together (Deuteronomy 21:20; Proverbs 23:20). What do these two things have in common? Both are motivated by greed. Weight problems give a clue to deep spiritual problems. Since we are spirit, we should always attack things from a spiritual view.

Excess weight brings idolatry; you begin to focus on yourself. We become so self-conscious about our excess flesh that craves attention and gets it, that we cannot serve God. Our self-esteem and confidence begin to wither, and we become poor examples of Jesus Christ. We spend so much time thinking about our fat that it begins to push out our time that should be spent on Jesus. We need this time so that we can be in perfect peace.

Ladies, can you imagine God sending us out on the front lines to fight in a raging war, when our main concern is if our fat knees (or other fat areas) are showing? Of course not!

Lord, teach us how to take care of these temples, according to Your will. Our bodies do not belong to us; they were bought and paid for with the precious blood of Jesus Christ. Proverbs 30:8 says, **"Remove far from me vanity and lies: give me neither poverty nor riches; feed me with food convenient for me."**

We must remain healthy to do the work of the Kingdom. Exercise, proper diet and rest are vital to our work.

As a wife, you may wonder, "Am I responsible for anything that is wrong with my husband's body?" Let's examine 1 Corinthians 7:3, 4:

> Let the husband render unto the wife due benevolence: and likewise also the wife unto the husband.
> The wife hath not power of her own body, but the husband: and likewise also the husband hath not power of his own body, but the wife.

The subject matter here is sexual, but it goes beyond sexuality. If your husband's body belongs to you, do you not take care of your possessions? If you bought a new suit, hat, gloves, coat, the works, wouldn't you attempt to keep them in good shape? We would not wear a new suit just any place. We wouldn't wear it to a dirty place, for it might get dirt on it. We wouldn't wear it to a fight, for it might get ripped. We would be careful to note that the atmosphere was right for a suit. We need to be just as careful with our husbands' bodies, so that no damage is done to them.

Take care of his body. Make sure it is strong and full of energy. Make sure the fuel going into his body enhances the decisions he has to make. One wife asked me, "How can I take care of my husband when he refuses to eat right?" You can start by caring. When I cook, it is my choice what I put in my food. I can start using less sugar, less white flour, bake instead of fry, steam vegetables, etc.

Going on a diet does not solve the spiritual problem. Most women become ashamed of their bodies because of allowing them to become overweight. Then we deprive our husbands from taking care of our bodies. We let the bad self-image, lack of discipline, low self-esteem, not to mention skin problems, back problems, hair problems, stomach problems, lack of energy and cellulite make us envious, jealous, liars and dishonest. We begin to look unto ourselves rather than unto Jesus. We eat for reward and comfort and out of boredom.

Jesus said, **Come unto me, all ye that labour and are heavy laden, and I will give you rest** (not food) (Matthew 11:28). Let us make sure that we are not making our bellies our god by giving more to our bellies than we give to God.

We can spend $20, $30, or $40 at a restaurant, yet complain about giving at church. We get caught up in greed and yes, we do become lovers of self more than lovers of God, lovers of money and we stop trusting God. The deeper the problem, the further away from God we get. We are drawn away by our own lusts.

We must begin to take care of ourselves for the sake of God's Kingdom. As women, we must care for our husband and children properly, according to the Word of God, not some man-made system of rules. The only solution is to *mature in the things of God.*

The Amplified Bible explains it this way:

Everything is permissible (allowable and lawful) for me; but not all things are helpful (good for me to do, expedient and profitable when considered with other things). Everything is lawful for me, but I will not become the slave of anything or be brought under its power.
1 Corinthians 6:12

The Curse of the Strong Woman   *Karen Clark-Green*

17

HAPPINESS FOR THE WHOLE PERSON

Usually, weight problems point to a deep psychological problem. Food is a self-satisfying, security replacement that sometimes is a way of screaming, "I am not happy!"

I have found that when I am in my place, everything works right. In *my place* means "fulfilling my call (career or ministry)." When I know I am in my place, I have more energy. The desire to fulfill myself with food is gone and I lose weight. In other words, I am happy and everything is in its place.

We are made up of three parts: spirit, soul and body, and each unit has distinct functions:

The spirit relates us to God and makes us conscious of him.

The soul relates us to ourselves and gives us consciousness.

The body relates us to our physical self.

It is important to understand these three elements: spirit, soul and body - as we culminate the understanding of our strength as women.

As children, we felt powerless to our adult authorities. Some of us carried that feeling over into our adult life and relationships. Until now, we have never been able to identify it.

What we must not overlook is the plan of God. But we must let go of the negatives that were added to our lives, even the safety of our own homes. We must choose to confess, forgive, release and go on with life.

Adam and Eve were not just the first man and woman on earth, they were also the first parents.

And Adam knew Eve his wife; and she conceived, and bare Cain, and said, I have gotten a man from the Lord.
And she again bare his brother Abel, and Abel was a keeper of sheep, but Cain was a tiller of the ground.
Genesis 4:1,2

In the story of Cain and Abel, Cain came against his brother and killed him. Whose fault was this? His parents? For the first time Adam and Eve had to work the land in order to survive. For the first time sweat, body aches, worry, fear and teenagers were introduced. The animals that were once friends became enemies. Stress entered the picture. How did they handle it? How did they capture this trial and error time of life?

We know how Cain and Abel turned out. Adam and Eve had no prior knowledge of how to be parents. I'm sure they tried to do what the Father had done with them, but things became very different after the fall.

> **And the Lord said unto Cain, Where is Abel thy brother? And he said, I know not: Am I my brother's keeper?**
> **And he said, What hast thou done? the voice of thy brother's blood crieth unto me from the ground.**
> **Genesis 4:9,10**

The Lord came to Cain and Abel concerning their actions. He did not go to Adam and Eve. The Lord did not say, "If your parents had done a better job, this would not have happened." At some point, you become responsible for yourself. Parents' imperfections are not to blame. Let go of the excuse of parental failure. Forgiveness always works because God has good plans for your life!

Soul Thinking

It is the area of your soul that has you thinking this way. The soul is inclined to the things of the past rather than things of the future. The soul is not quick to move on.

As adults, many of us have dreams of present events that take place in the homes that we grew up in. Maybe you hear your favorite high school record which triggers memories from your past. Or, you smell that same smell from a certain time in your life; an old boyfriend's cologne or grandma's apple pie. Suddenly memories flood your mind and you are back in those times. The soul may need to reflect to glean all the treasures of those past events. Learn from them, don't run from them, for running from your past will keep you stuck there.

The soul is involved in things of this world, while your spirit is the "real you."

Menopause

A woman who has learned who she is and loves herself, develops more beauty as she grows older. The attack on our female power has always made it seem as though the changes that take place with our bodies are negative.

We all grew up hearing about "the curse" that was bestowed upon us because of Eve. So, young flowering girls regretfully anticipate the beginning of womanhood, waiting to suffer through the monthly pain of menstruation. The wives' tales in reference to the agony of child birth has left a fear of getting pregnant on many young women.

It is time to celebrate the budding of our bodies into the beauty of maturity. We must talk to our daughters so they understand that this is not a bad thing happening to them, but a Godly, beautiful thing.

Middle-aged women fear their female attractiveness will fade as they etch towards forty, fifty, sixty, and so forth. Have we been fooled! Mid-life crises should be labeled, "Mid-life awakening." This is a wonderful time when we realize that we are not little girls but grown, responsible women. We begin to reflect and evaluate and realize that it is time to get down to business. It is a time when our hormones are not bossing us around in our soulish area. Actually, we begin to balance out as our estrogen level drops, taking us into menopause.

There are other hormones that rise at this time, like androgen and testosterone, and we actually become more levelheaded.

Imagine having heard all of your life that:

- Menopause brings freedom to you as a woman.

- Menopause is not a disease that has to be treated, but a powerful, full blooming time of your life.

- New beginnings come with menopause.

It is true that we must take better care of our bodies as we go into menopause. Our bodies tell us what we need and what we don't need at this stage of life.

The symptoms of menopause can be controlled through diet. High fat diets will not keep you living to be a hundred. So your body says, "You have eaten the wrong foods in the past. Listen to what I tell you to put into your body to keep you healthy, and I will keep you going."

Society says, through commercials, magazines, etc., that a woman's value is through her sexual attractiveness and the ability to bear children. As we grow older, society does not say that we become distinguished and knowledgeable. Menopausal women have heard the unspoken message that their desirability to men has now come to a halt.

If you are a menopausal woman, *you are in your fullness of power and beauty.* There is nothing worse than the lack of knowledge. Prepare yourself, find out the pros and cons of this time of life. It is true that most mothers don't inform us, but stop being afraid of what you don't know! Find out the facts and use them to your advantage.

What does a menopausal women look like?

> **And it came to pass, when he was come near to enter into Egypt, that he said unto Sarai his wife, Behold now, I know that thou art a fair woman to look upon:**
> **Therefore it shall come to pass, when the Egyptians shall see thee, that they shall say, This is his wife: and they will kill me, but they will save thee alive.**
> **Say, I pray thee, thou art my sister: that it may be well with me for thy sake; and my soul shall live because of thee.**
> **And it came to pass, that, when Abram was come into Egypt, the Egyptians beheld the woman that she was very fair.**
> **The princes also of Pharaoh saw her, and commended her before Pharaoh: and the woman was taken into Pharaoh's house.**
> **Genesis 12:11-15**

Please keep in mind that Sarai was almost ninety years old at this time. Abram knew that she was a knockout! He knew that she was so attractive and desirable that once the Pharaoh and these princes saw how beautiful she was, they would kill him to get her.

Don't let others decide who you are and what you should look like. If you decide to die, your body will beat you to it. *Live and look the best you can all of your life!*

You can make this powerful phase of your life the most exciting and glamorous. Eat healthy, get proper rest, start new projects and change your mind about who you thought you were.

The Curse of the Strong Woman   *Karen Clark-Green*

18

WALKING IN AUTHORITY

On January 14, 1996, I was preparing for the Martin Luther King Celebration at Cuyahoga Community College in Cleveland, Ohio. I was to perform the world premiere debut of Delores White's composition, "Give Birth to the Dream," a work composed for narrator, soprano and orchestra. Ms. White's lyrics are taken from Maya Angelou's poem, "On the Pulse of Morning."

The day I received the music score, I was eager to read it and add it to my repertoire. I was flattered when my friend, Conductor William Slocum, considered me to perform this wonderful piece of music. As I read the lyrics of the excerpts from Ms. Angelou's poem, it seemed as if God had picked each phrase that applied to my life. It was exactly where I was at the time, discovering who, what and why I exist.

All of this brought back memories of nine years earlier, as I prepared for the same event, with the same orchestra, in the same place, with Maya Angelou as the featured artist. I knew only God could arrange such a thing, but what happened to me in these nine years?

I very dramatically rehearsed the words from the poem that I would narrate and the words from the poem that I would sing. My prayer was that I would not become so emotional that I would cry or get so involved that I would forget I was on stage.

Literally, I was declaring my new beginning! This was to be the first performance of the "real me." I had gained new insights, emotions, hopes and dreams, new people in my life and old pains out of my life. I was so grateful to God.

Why was this personal accomplishment being affirmed with so many witnesses?

My designer, Jeanetta Pugh, had made a gown for the performance nine years earlier that I knew I was also to wear for this special event. Maya Angelou's presence was there, full and alive, recreating a past event that had brought me to this present day.

"Are you nervous?" she asked. "Yes, a little," I answered. I had not realized the total impact of January 18, 1987, and I knew I had to absorb all the jewels from that event. The clock, the stage, the orchestra, everything faded into that January day as if we were whizzed through eternity backwards for a brief space in time.

Once again, I felt the overwhelming sense of her presence. I listened as she entered her bag of wisdom. I had not realized that she was making me dig deeper within my spirit to find myself. I did not realize that she was helping me to get in position to walk into myself, down a prepaid, prepared road that had my name on it. I was embarking on a nine-year journey that would bring me full circle back to the beginning.

Her piercing, warm, commanding, sweet words of how to take over the stage and deposit hope into my audience brought me back to the present. I listened intently as I was lifted once again into another realm, knowing that I had a message to deliver that had to make the wood, the curtains, the walls and even the instruments listen attentively

Emotion gripped me as I walked on stage. My heart throbbed with ministry that was to be delivered through this magnificent work. As I began to speak the poem, "A rock, a river, a tree," I saw faces of people who were looking for hope. I saw faces of people who had found their way into my heart and had deposited new feelings there. I saw faces of people who had caused me pain but forced me to grow. I saw my four beautiful children who are an extension of me. I saw my future, and I saw the road on which to travel there.

I could feel the heart of my audience, and I felt responsible for their feelings at that moment. As I completed the narration of the poem with the intertwining interludes of the orchestra, I invited the audience to join me on the next level. Maya Angelou's poem beckoned:

The Curse of the Strong Woman   Karen Clark-Green

> Across the wall of the world
> A river sings a beautiful song,
> Come, rest here by my side.

As I moved center stage to sing, I don't remember walking there, I was just there. I felt vulnerable, exposed and transparent. I knew that each member of the audience was being prepared to receive the personal message that their hearts needed to hear and I began to sing:

> I am a tree, planted by the river,
> which will not be moved.
> I am a rock, planted by the river,
> which will not be moved.

Delores White's music greatly complimented Maya's words. I knew that I had to be very careful in interpreting this combination to the audience. A couple of times I felt my voice waver, I thought that I might cry, but the message had to be delivered for the sake of the people, and for me.

As I reached the section that spoke of the pain of my history and facing it with courage which would keep me from having to live it again, I felt deliverance. I began to feel the instructions of what to do with my new beginning, the dream that I had to resurrect.

> Take it into the palm of your hands,
> Mold it into the shape of your most private need.
> Sculpt it into the image of your most public self,
> And give birth to the dream.

Maya Angelou

Conclusion
Elements in Review

Here is a summary of the key elements we have discussed in this book about enhancing our womanhood:

1. Know who you are and develop it.

You have a call of God on your life, a purpose for being in the earth - more than just washing dishes and birthing babies. Society has measured our value by the success of nurturing or taking care of others. This is an innate quality that comes with being a woman and by no means measures our value.

2. Believe in yourself.

David had to encourage himself in the Lord (I Samuel 30:6). Don't wait for others to agree or see what you see, for it may not happen. There are times when no one believed in anything I was doing, except Jesus and me!

When trials come to test your faith, you will fail every time if you are depending on someone else. Gossip, judging, false accusations and loss of friends come with the territory when you are called to do great things. Get over it, or these things will hinder you from becoming all God wants you to be.

3. Your life is complete.

Everything you need to be a success is already within you. You may need to do some fine-tuning or get more education to bring your gift to fruition, but the gift itself is already within you.

God starts at the end, the finished work. Then He places you at the beginning and pulls you into Himself. You have to keep moving to grasp this. Every step you take is a step in purpose, ordered by God. When there is no movement taking place, you are stuck; and you will stay in your situation until movement starts again.

4. *Answer the call to the high place.*

You are the queen of the earth, so don't just settle for anything. Go for the gold! Allow your way of thinking to be changed. When challenges come, learn all you can from them. Then use them as fuel to propel you to the next level. Keep growing and adding to your womanhood.

In a relationship, it is dangerous when only one partner is growing or changing. *Grow together,* allowing change to take place in both of you, or the passion in the relationship will subside.

5. *Stay connected to God.*

Remember, you were created special, hand-crafted, a special design, that only God could master. *Your power lies in knowing who you are as a woman.* You are spirit, soul and body, but the "real you" is your spirit. Your power comes from within rather than from without.

Women who see femininity as weakness are stuck in a self-supporting, self-protecting mode. This will cause you to overwork in every area, blocking out your need to be secure enough, to trust enough, to relax and become "all female." Seek help to get in touch with your femininity again!

Bibliography

Allender, Dan B. *The Wounded Heart,* Navpress Books, Colorado Springs, CO, 1990.

Crenshaw, Mary Ann. *Natural Way to Super Beauty,* David McKay, New York, NY 1974.

Evans, Jimmy. *Marriage on the Rock,* Vincom, Inc., Tulsa, OK, 1992.

Foley, Denise and Nechas, Eileen. *Women's Encyclopedia of Emotional Healing,* Rodole Press, Emmaus, PA, 1993.

Forward, Susan and Torres, Joan. *Men Who Hate Women and The Women Who Love Them,* Bantam Books, New York, 1986.

McIntosh, Ron. *Keep the Flame Burning,* Vincom, Inc., Tulsa, OK, 1992.

Modern Woman's Medical Encyclopedia. Doubleday, Garden City, NY, 1966.

Sprinkle, Patricia. *Women Who Do Too Much,* Zondervan Publishing Co., Grand Rapids, MI, 1973.

Yancey, Philip. *Where Is God When It Hurts,* Zondervan